Excerpt from *The Third M Grace from*

My story is not for everyone to hear it. My story is for those whose desire for Heaven on Earth is a natural force lifting them to new planes of experience. My story is for those who understand that a mother's heart is valuable, has worth, is necessary in the unfolding awareness of portions of Jesus the Christ's and the Lady Mary Magdalene's story. My story is for those who desire absolution from earthly woes, and are willing to shift their own energetic frequencies to support this. My story is for everyone who desires to be his or her full potential. My story is meant to awaken you to your own significance through deepening your awareness of the truth of those biblical times and by activating your own abilities more strongly for assisting in the Creation of Heaven on Earth.

My story is for those of you who are tired of the same old pendulum swing of duality, who want to experience Heaven as Earth NOW, who enjoy listening within for their Truth signal.

My story is for all ages and times. My story is encompassing, weaving through and protecting your story. My story is about the giving and receiving of love on all levels. My story is without end, for it is of the Infinite. My story rests within your story, as you unfold your own gifts and nature wisely. My story accrues its wisdom through the compilation and interweaving of all stories of reclamation inviting personal truth to come together with the Absolute and Eternal.

My story is simply one story with many wings to impart truth through many angles of perambulation. And it is trying to speak through your story in such a way that it might uplift, sustain and empower you to tell the power of your own inner world's story, and to keep you engaged with your Higher Nature throughout your time here on Earth.

My story is unveiled through your willingness to discern it as just a piece of the larger puzzle of creating Heaven on Earth. My story is to impart to you the meaning, the significance that will grow your awareness more fully in these new times through new awareness of the meaning, the significance, of the old times.

My story is my story, available to accept or reject as you please. But it cannot leave you untouched, unmoved, unchanged, because it begins with your piece of the puzzle for creating Heaven on Earth in it. And it is multi-layered with energies for your Highest Good.

My story is helpful for those who choose to live their lives more fully, as sentient creatures on Heaven as Earth, and to remind you of your own Divine Nature.

My story is willing to support your story in shining Truth's Light over all creation, and to support the growth of Light here for all.

My story is a doorway for all who choose to enter. Let us enter together now.

THE THIRD MARY

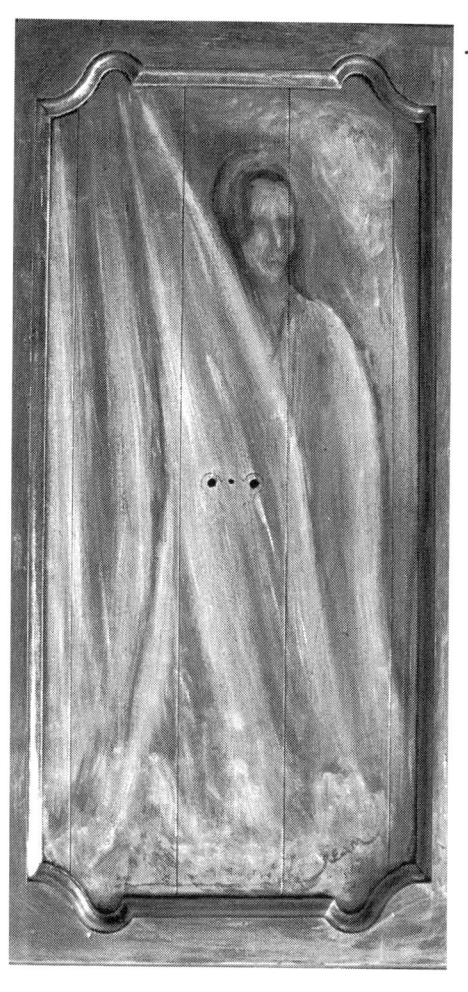

To Mary Angela,
with Much
Love & Gratitude!
Roxely

Also by Roslyn Elena McGrath

*Goddess Heart Rising: Paintings, Poems & Meditations
for Activating Your Divine Potential*

Creative Wisdom Cards & Meditations for Personal Growth

A New Radiance: Chakra Blessings from the Divine Feminine
Meditation CD

THE THIRD MARY

55 Messages for Empowering Truth, Peace & Grace
from the Mother of Mary Magdalene

Roslyn Elena McGrath

Chrysaetos Press

Copyright © 2014 by Roslyn McGrath. All rights reserved.

No part of this book may be reproduced or transmitted in any form or by any means, including written, electronic, recording, or photocopying, or by any information storage and retrieval system without written permission of the author, except in the case of brief quotations with proper credit given to the author.

The contents herein are a personal account and not intended in any way to be construed as historically documented or researched information.

Published by Chrysaetos Press

Contact the publisher for book sales at:

P.O. Box 583, Marquette, MI 49855

(906) 228-9097

www.TheThirdMary.com

Printed in the U.S.A.

Editing: Tyler Tichelaar

Art: Roslyn Elena McGrath

(Half-title page - *Mo-Ray Angelica;* back page - *Matriarchal Madonna*)

Photography: Kristine Granger

ISBN-13: 978-0615990224

ISBN-10: 0615990223

1. Body/Mind/Spirit 2. Ancient Mysteries & Controversial Knowledge

To my mother, Alma,

to the Light within each of us,

and to you.

Foreword

After years of internal searching, countless trainings, spiritual workshops, and processes on the heart and soul's evolution, I have come to the realization there is a beauty, a light, a rhythm and an integrity that shines when the soul expresses itself. Reading *The Third Mary* enfolded me in that dance and embraced me with ancient truths and hidden secrets never before revealed. Tidbits from the lives of Mary the Elder's daughter, the Lady Mary Magdalene, Jesus the Christ, Judas, Mother Mary, daughter Martha, and other players from 2000 years ago are presented authentically, in a light that is unique and also helps to bridge longstanding questions.

As any parent can tell you, there are joys and challenges with raising any child, yet there is a complexity that comes with raising a child so conscious of her divinity and purpose. Mary the Elder shares her story through Roslyn as only she can tell it. Written with bravery, integrity, honesty and heart, I find *The Third Mary* to be a gift to us all. No matter what your beliefs, you will be led to the place that many give little consideration to: your soul. I thank Roslyn McGrath for going so deep within herself to bring Mary the Elder forward. Her story is a treasure we've longed for. We eagerly await what she has to share with us next.

Joy Regina Melchezidek
Founder and Executive Director of Tee-Shirts for Peace
Author of . . . *And God Woke Up (Rewriting My Story)*
Host of *Joy of Union*
Channel, teacher, and heart/soul facilitator

Acknowledgments

I am forever grateful to Flo Aeveia Magdalena for sharing her visions of Mary Magdalene's life so beautifully through her book *I Remember Union,* and for sharing so much of the meaning of this life through her creation and directing of Soul Support Systems; to Ward Cole for emphatically handing me my first copy of *I Remember Union,* to Joy Regina Melchezidek for encouraging my communications with Mary Magdalene's mother; and to her, Stephen O'Dell, Nicole Walton, and Maria Formolo for their invaluable keen insights, edits, feedback and heart-filled support of this work.

Many thanks go to Tyler Tichelaar for his expert editing and for always being such a pleasure to work with, and to Kristine Granger for so generously and beautifully photographing my art.

I also wish to thank Susan Shaver, who long ago gave credence to my subtle impressions before I did myself, and who gave me my first experience of LaHo-Chi's energetic healing; to Kim Regnitz for twice initiating me into LaHo-Chi; and to Michael David Lawrence and Dan and Rio Watson for their foundational roles in making this possible, as this energy practice has helped bring forth my ability to receive the messages in this book.

Special thanks also to my writing "coven," whose deep listening, friendship and examples of their own authentic voices help me to better hear my own voice and the voices of those who speak through me; to my parents for providing the foundation for me to become who I am; to Auriel Coleman, for her part in helping me to live my mission; to all those who have and are "waking up" with me, as we spur one another forward, whether we consciously know each other or not; to the Soul Support Systems community and all who endeavor to live Heaven on Earth; and to my husband Kevin for all of his continuous loving support.

And my heart is full of appreciation to Mary of Niza, mother of Mary Magdalene, for sharing her courage, commitment, wisdom and love through these messages, and for making herself available to us all.

Introduction

Who is the mother of Mary Magdalene? Why did she share a series of messages to the world through me? And why should you read them?

In the late '90s, a dear friend was so smitten with *I Remember Union* by Flo Aeveia Magdalena that he was giving copies away to friends, saying, "You've got to read this book!" I did and was totally enthralled. It retells Mary Magdalene's role as Jesus the Christ's twin flame and a vital partner in their mission to help catalyze the creation of Heaven on Earth, to be completed in our time. The book shares the living presence of these beings and of the Divine Realms. It holds keys that may lead to tapping into one's personal relationship to biblical times and part in our planetary evolution.

For me, this has much to do with Mary Magdalene's mother. Although mentioned only briefly in the book, an awareness of her stayed with me. By the time I reached the end of Mary Magdalene's story, my inner guidance told me, "And you were her mother." Over the years, each time I reread or thought about the book, I would hear again, "And you were her mother."

How could this be? I have experienced enough diverse past life overlays and memories, and their influence on this lifetime, to feel confident that we do "recycle" into a series of physical life experiences from our eternal and ongoing existence in the Higher Realms, allowing us to gain greater wisdom and reconnect in new ways with those we love. But could even a past version of me have played such a key role as to help raise such an incredible being as Mary Magdalene?

Perhaps some of you who are parents have felt this same awe at the empowered, wonderful beings your children have become and also wondered how you came to be their parent. I believe we make some key soul agreements before each lifetime about the kinds of roles we will play with each other. So I've come to accept that in some capacity, I made a soul agreement to tap into this one.

And I am not the only one. As described in *I Remember Union,* each of the key players in biblical times is part of a group of 144,000 souls, all of whom would be involved in the creation of Heaven on Earth 2,000 years later. Mary Magdalene's mother has told me I am one of seventy souls currently having human lifetimes here that all carry aspects of her.

My experience is that the further we explore the Higher Realms, the more amorphous the concept of identity becomes, as we experience more of our interconnectedness and oneness, allowing us to access a potentially limitless range of consciousness and experiences.

So who *is* Mary Magdalene's mother? As you'll discover in reading her messages, she, as we each ultimately are, is a multi-dimensional and eternal being who was very consciously honored and privileged to help guide and prepare the young Mary Magdalene to step into her empowered role. She is also a very compassionate, clear, grounded guide, available to help each of us step into our individual missions in the Grand Design for creating Heaven on Earth.

You'll find her descriptions of herself and her specific names are gradually unveiled over the course of this book. As author Ted Andrews put it so well, "The name, if understood and used correctly, summons the character and essences that it represents."[1] We are each so much more than we appear outwardly. Mary Magdalene's mother extends many aspects of herself through these messages in order ultimately to awaken greater consciousness of our own.

And her story is not only that of a Heavenly being, which we all are at our core, but also that of a very *human* being. She raised a daughter who consciously faced and met huge challenges that have greatly affected our planetary experience. She played an active and important role in carrying on the Goddess tradition, and also, by our current standards, lived a suppressed existence in a relatively brutal, patriarchal society.

She has remained hidden from public awareness for eons, while observing and participating from the Unseen Realms. But now, as we stand on the threshold of quite literally experiencing Heaven on Earth, it is time for her, the mother of Mary Magdalene, Mary the Elder, to become visible, as it is time for each one of us to become visible to ourselves and one another as our larger beings, our true Divine potential embodied in physical form.

Initially, when I would tap into my connection with her, I'd experience a huge well of emotion related to the personal challenges of that lifetime. It felt potentially overwhelming to me, so I chose not to explore it further. And I believed I couldn't dare tell anyone about this past life connection.

---

[1] Andrews, Ted, *The Sacred Power In Your Name*, Llewellyn Publications, St. Paul, Minnesota, 1998, p.10.

INTRODUCTION

But nearly fifteen years after first reading *I Remember Union*, the topic began coming up more frequently. Finally, during a conversation with Joy Regina Melchezidek, I felt compelled to share my connection to Mary Magdalene's mother. This became an invaluable turning point when Joy strongly suggested I dialogue with her and find out her story. I responded vehemently, "No! I don't want to!" But as soon as I'd heard the suggestion, I began hearing Mary Magdalene's mother's voice in my head. The next day, a short poem from her came to me when I awoke, and about a week later, I began taking down the messages that comprise this book.

Interestingly, that day was August 15th, which I later discovered is Mother Mary's Feast Day. And on Sept. 21st, the Fall Equinox, Mary Magdalene's mother revealed that Mary was also her primary name in her biblical lifetime. She has since told me this was her approximate birthdate in that lifetime.

For me, this has been a very personal journey of integration and becoming more visible, as I continue to absorb the multi-level energies and information of *The Third Mary's* messages, to make her voice available to myself and others, and to paint images of various aspects of her. As will be clear from the first messages, I was certainly leery of the process initially, though I soon came to look forward to this scribing as the most meaty, important part of my day. It was the first thing I would do each morning for the majority of a sixty-eight-day period. Though over the past fifteen years I have channeled other high spiritual energies, and occasionally humans who've transitioned, the Third Mary's energy is more solid, immediately available to me and very compatible with my own, though definitely different from it. There is a distinctive rhythm and quality to her sentence structure, and she is quite exact about her wording. I would listen as carefully as I could for each word, several of which I'd never heard of before that she would spell out for me. And I never knew what was coming next. Each time she shifted topics, I would feel a sudden shift in the energy coming through, as I felt the vibration of everything she described move through me.

And I definitely preferred some parts of this material over others. When I began this scribing, I assumed it would predominantly share stories of Mary Magdalene and biblical times, and was chomping at the bit for the "preparation period" to be over, certain that this wouldn't require more than a few messages of introduction. I had no idea this manuscript would continue to weave past, present and future into a personal and planetary preparation for the incredible new human experience of which we're on the threshold. But eventually I "got it" and greatly anticipated receiving each morning's message.

Still, there are parts which took more of my patience, (you'll know them by her repeated expressions of thanks for this patience at these points!), and which I felt I had to move through, whether I could consciously comprehend them fully or not, to get to my favorite parts, the earthly stories of biblical times. And when the Third Mary would speak of Mary Magdalene, Jesus, and Mother Mary, it always felt like a great breaking out into more light to me, and I treasured these sharings immensely.

The messages presented here are encoded with frequencies for our evolvement at many levels. So, though there are parts I believe are more suited to brains different from my own and parts which appear quite specific and personal to me, as well as briefly mundane (such as suggesting I go eat my breakfast!), and even a few words that may not be in any dictionary, the Third Mary's fifty-five messages of visions, fables, biblical times, spiritual practices and advice are shared here verbatim to the best of my consciousness's ability to accomplish this, so they might impact each of us in the way they're intended, on personal, planetary and multi-dimensional levels.

You'll notice her refer to "you" regularly. Does she mean "me," "you" specifically, or all of us? My sense of that would morph as the particular message continued, and I've come to believe it's likewise intended this way in order to function on these multiple levels, helping to break down the concept of separation and move us toward more consistent awareness that we are truly all one.

I believe the essence and the purpose of the Third Mary's messages is to prepare us specifically to live more fully from this oneness consciousness, the union of souls that continues to include the diversity of all our aspects, vital to the era which we are on the verge of stepping into.

May reading this material help activate and prepare you to step forward as your full, original and unique, Divinely human self, as we come into our greater wholeness together.

Roslyn Elena Angeliese McGrath

Introduction from the Mother of Mary Magdalene, 8/7/13

I was the one who showed her how to send,

I was the one who showed her how to send.

I was the one who told her not to bend.

I was the one who told her not to bend.

I was the one who showed her

Love has no end.

Love has no end.

Love has no end.

THE THIRD MARY

8/7/13

What else could I do but what I had to? I knew she would absolve all wrongs, mend them at a level that I never knew. I also knew the cost, and that my job was never to judge her for choosing a road so hard, though it broke my heart thousands of times over. I thank her for changing the world, and challenging me to love through the pain, through the hardship of one who knows the bitter taste of sacrifice for long term, all-worlds gain. The energy was so heavy then. You would not recognize your world. You think it is difficult now with suicides, drug addictions, plagues. Our times were more brutal, mercy far less common, our thirst for Heaven more prevalent because of this.

I know you have to go now. I will write with you again. My story must be told. I thank you.

La Magdalena

8/15/13

It is time for my story to be told. I understand you are loathe to do it. It is not my energy that causes this; it is your own. You do not understand the purpose or value, just the sorrow. Yet all is well.

I am the Mother of Mary Magdalene, as she is known historically, as you know. I cannot stay quiet when I know the world requires my story too. I am the Keeper of the Records of humankind's mystical, pre-history and of several aspects of "biblical" time as well.

There are many lessons here for those immersed in theology, as well as those gripped in conflicts with the caverns of life. I am a staunch supporter of all that goes well in the world, and an understanding heart to all that does not. I know where my people go, and where they came from. It is interesting that you have my tale to tell when you know your own so sparsely.

I trust that you can "get out of your own way" enough to allow my truth to emerge, and are understanding enough to accept all the wonders it can bring. It is, without exception, a truly unique tale of foresight, apprehension, commitment and follow-through of unprecedented proportions in your human tells.

I am an aspect of your own human nature as yet untouched by city life, modern rudiments, and late twentieth century and beyond developments. When you "sing" with me, your joys become sorrows and your sorrows joys, because of the intense nature of Truth and your response to it. Over time, this will balance out, and your original fears and concerns become meaningless.

I am showing you an aspect of your own tale as well, which will resolve much that has been concerning you. It is enough that you know this for now – **I am your mother** and the mother of all who came before you, in the sense that I choose nurturance and love of Truth before all else.

And I am carrying Records of a Time before your birth that has many implications for it.

There is a great evolution happening now throughout your towns and cities, within your hearts and minds. Your dogs feel it too. All of nature responds to your actions, within and without. And they are recounted within the legends of your birth and recorded in the Annals of the One-Is-All-Is-One.

I am a Way Show-er as well. I show the way to beneficence and beauty through the human mud of apparent decay and loss. And I am well aware of its impact on each one of you. I am always caring and showing what is required to reveal itself next for your own Highest Good. And I am an example of the Oneness harbingering Truth for all those who desire it, and require it, though there are many who think they do not. Yet they will come to this, and I to them, as well.

You may call me by my first name now, Mirandella. Yes, I know this is not Judaical, but it suits me well. I am a mirror and Miracle of the Truth, developing soundly throughout your world. I am trusting your forethought to examine all you have held in your heart so far, hold it up to the Light and see what it reflects, where this Light shines through, and where it does not, so that you can naturally allow the latter to go, to fall away, as you concentrate upon the Light core.

It is well that you write with me at this time, because many opportunities are about to arise in your world, and you will desire a firm hand with foresight to guide you.

I am knowing you are longing for the Truth and the Light and the Way to be apparent on the Earth, willingly followed by all, and for all to embrace this knowing with Delight. This is not likely to occur in the way and with the speed that you would most desire; however, your request is known and it does assist. The Truth will be known and it will be followed and elaborated upon in due course, within (and beyond), your own human lifetime.

That is not to say that you cannot experience *all* of the joys of it right now. And in truth, it does allow the process to "speed up" within your earthly annals of time.

Portals are available to see into and know the Truth of the Oneness faster and its delights upon the Earth. And I know that there are those around whom it is said, "Light, Love and Laughter lead the way," and it is good.

Yet you find me heavy within yourself. Why is this so? Are you afraid of knowing something so important and healing as this truth? No, Dear One. You are not. You are simply resounding with the Heart of the Truth and responding very emotionally to it. And you are still healing from the wounds emotionally as yet unresolved from the time period from which I am known.

This is enough for now. We shall speak/write again on the morrow.

Amen, with loving joy, Your Own Truth Mother of the Magdalene

8/16/13

I am the Mother of Mary Magdalene, as well as others. She came to me in a dream before her birth and asked me if I'd be willing to consecrate her to the Goddess. I said, "Of course." She asked me again. I said, "I will." She asked once more. I said, "I must."

It was always this way with her, checking for understanding, searching for Truth, with substance and integrity. I knew when we began our lessons on the Earth plane that she was like no other born to me. She sang rhymes before she would walk. She listened to and watched intently all that was going on around her. She could distinguish shapes and colors long before my others could. She was a marvel. And very headstrong. Once she took it into her head to do something, there was no rest until she had accomplished it.

She was a sunny child too, of cheerful disposition. She would often smile at others when they were down, in such a way that they warmed to her rather than gathering in their fierceness, as often is the way when one tries to assist another that does not want it. They sensed her compassion and responded to this. She knew the ways of the Goddess long before I began to teach her, but she always wanted more of this, and would sit by my knees for hours at a time, when we could do so, drinking in the sound of my voice and the concepts played out in our mind's eyes.

I knew as soon as I began a lesson that it would be hours before she would allow me to finish. She was very set in her desires. And she wanted Truth even more than Love or approval. And she lived her truth quite beautifully, as you are well aware.

I am telling you all this so you will know more about me as well, for I was shaped by her shaping in ways that I was unaware of at the time. It is truly the task for which I was born. All else falls away in comparison, though I will be sharing other parts of my life as well. Still all points come back to this, my one true calling that calls me still.

For it is my time to shine, as well as your own. Within the depths of each being, there lies a code, a code which can only be activated by one's life purpose and those destined to trigger it.

I am coming to you with a mission relevant to your own, a mission that asks each one of us to look within for the power that moves worlds, turns the earth and stars, and brings us what we each seek in our own fashion, the knowing and experience of Oneness, which is the Truth beyond all Truths. Heaven is meant to be lived upon this earth plane, once we have explored falsehood truly. For it must be chosen rightly, knowing its alternative and desiring it no more. I am grateful that I did my part in living my design and I can attest to the Truth within all nature. I am above board in this regard. And I am Truly knowing the Oneness in you. It behooves you to move into this state of grace more clearly now, for the levels have accelerated and that which is not accelerating with it may be left behind, or rather, need to work itself much harder in order to make up this difference.

I am aware of the pain that many feel about the evolution, the coming times, the changes that they perceive within themselves and upon the planet. Yet there is much to enjoy, to celebrate, for the parting with the ways of man are coming soon, and the ideas of Heaven can now allow us to choose the only true alternative, the ways of Oneness, which Christ did much to prepare us for so long ago.

Mary Magdalene worked in tandem with him in this, so many years ago. Yet it had to be hidden, for it was not yet time to reveal her Light. Mankind was in great conflict and the time of women was soon submerged. It is coming to the forefront again, in order to allow the Oneness, the merging, to come into fruition. Your work is an indelible part of this, for you are allowing yourself to speak for and represent aspects of the Goddess. It is well that you allow yourself to move through all the energies that you do, for you are a Way Show-er as well. And I do delight in your sharing of the Truth.

I am always amazed by how each one of us takes center stage, as it were, in our turn, yet never believe it as our own location, but that of the Oneness that moves its spotlight on to the next and the next and the next, 'til all is known in the fullness of the Oneness that unites all, *without exception*.

Even your own displays of Truth pale before this knowing. And yet they are crucial to its performance here on Earth. Our loving and living know no quarter that they may guide us to ever greater acknowledgment of the One-Is-All-Is-One.

And so it is. I will speak with you again this way on the morrow. I am ever loving you and your soul's journey.

I am the Mother of Mary Magdalene, and I come to show you Truth through my own story.

8/17/13

I am the Mother of Mary Magdalene. I come to you because you chose to, and because I am you. I experience much of your involvement with the Earth plane, as you experience a fair part of my own. I am waiting upon the final changes for all to be revealed. And I am understanding the need to be prepared for such, so I am sharing much of my story through you now.

I am awakening too. I have "slumbered," in a manner of speaking, for eons, though I have an awareness of all that has surfaced during this time. And I am certain that this time is the time for experiencing all that we truly are, all aspects of our real, true selves, and that I am as much a part of you as you are of me. So I am investigating this time and place more thoroughly than most others. And I am finding much wanting here of certain aspects of our nature. I have come to teach you how to cherish your own unique Divinity, how to carry it out in the world without exception, and how to love unconditionally. You are a model student because you have no barriers to my teachings of any note, and because your desire to learn such is as strong as mine is to share it with you.

I understand the shortcomings of experiencing through this time and place alone; therefore, I am also helping you to expand your ability to see/experience multiple planes of reality at once. Your dogs understand that I am purposely teaching you this so you can interact more fully with them and all species as well.

I am coming to you at this time because circumstances allow it, you are welcoming it, and ultimately, because it is the Divine Timing we both have chosen on very deep levels of our beings. I trust that this is the sort of experience you can totally share with others, for it is meant for many of them as well.

I told you I am the Mother of Mary Magdalene. That is true. You are also her Mother, and all are, every time they foster the ability of another to "shine their light," as it were, more fully. I cannot explain the depth of service that this can require, for you know it well, and, without exception, it changes your ability to shine your own light more fully as well.

I am noticing many of the events you are experiencing upon the Earth plane now as part and parcel of the magnificent Earth changes now manifesting and also of your own human brains, their quirks and fears. It would behoove all of you now to examine your motives more clearly for all that you do, to dispel any residue of times past that are unworthy of your True self. For the time is coming very soon now to begin truly anew. And the more clearly you can know and carry your Highest hopes and dreams forward, without barnacles of old unwanteds clinging to them, the more fully and harmoniously you can experience your version of Heaven on Earth.

I am watching you now and I am wondering, "What are you waiting for? What holds you back? When the Truth is so simple and clear." Yet I understand the exigencies of a mortal lifetime, the cares and woes that build up because of them, and the incomplete nature of each one's understanding of his or her own humanity.

I am one who delves deep into the forefront of human historical aims and does what she can to set them aright. I have watched now for eons and participated from a great distance, yet one could not care more deeply than I for all that you all are going through, and all of the trials and tribulations that have come before.

When I myself walked the Earth plane, I wasn't caring quite so much for the benefits of All, though I knew they would come from the process of my work with my daughter, Mary Magdalene, and her work with Jesus the Christ, and their work as it has unfolded through countless others, time untold. I have suffered greatly in this process, yet always known the best was yet to come, and it still is. It was more than worth every agony, and I did what I could at the time to relieve myself of the burdens of my troubled mind by dwelling upon all the positive outcomes to come.

I was not alone in my work. There were many others who supported me in it, and supported young Mary in her learnings. It is safe to say that the community of women with me at that time, as well as future women and key men, both past and future, were instrumental in all that has come to pass. And I am yet sharing the knowing that we are all well related in this and that *you* are knowing you are among them in the now.

When the time is ripe, I will share my teachings more fully with others. For now, it is enough to know that you are with me, faithfully inscribing the words as you hear them.

I am knowing that you have much work before you on this Earth plane, good work that will fulfill you in ways you've yet to dream of. And I am understanding your impatience to get on with it, to have it all out there.

Just remember, a bit at a time is best. Some bits will appear "larger" than others. All bits are equally available and interesting, as well as life-shine making. I ask for your patience as my own story unfolds as well, for the telling of it in its own time and way is crucial.

That is enough for this now. I bid you adieu and wish you well in every moment and aspect.

I am the Mother of Mary Magdalene, and I know you well.

8/18/13

I am the Mother of Mary Magdalene. I come to you because you are one of my soldiers, in the sense that you offer the opportunity to move my vision, my purpose, forward.

I can tell that you are of like mind, in some areas more than others, of course. And while you cannot be expected to know all that I will tell, you have a foreshadowing perhaps. I trust your sense of Truth and dignity will bring forward all that I desire of this recounting. And I know full well and am very aware that all of this self-creating is ultimately of Good, of Truth. What I mean by that is all of the world's computations, calculations, masturbations, all of the fracas of life, will ultimately boil down to one thing – UNION. Though it appears to be of a far-off time, it is not. It is safe to say that the door is wide open and that humankind, collectively, has a foot in the doorway, a toe on the threshold, and there is no going back now, only forward, into the Light.

I trust your ability to represent me truly as I am, without dressing up or hazzerah. I am well aware of the opportunity for growth available through my make-up, my disposition, as it were, my vibrational content. You feel my sense of inner authority grow in yourself, do you not?

And I am trusting that it is yet possible for us to divulge together some of the secrets of the Universe, in the sense that all of us are part and parcel of this process, yet some of us are nudged forward to turn the tumblers into place, so that the door may yield without force, with a sense of ease and Grace. You are well aware of the power of Grace. It moves throughout your being and motivates all that you do toward being in Harmony with your greater Self and in Union with All-That-Is. I am avoiding discussing my role in your background for now. There will be a time where all will be revealed to you of this, but for now, suffice it to say that I could easily have been your Soul Mother as well.

I am happy that we are connecting in this way now and I am sure there will be much Light to carry forward in the days, weeks, and months ahead.

There are many opportunities before you. Which doors to open? Which doors to close? I have allowed myself to signify which are of more Light to you by a pattern of sparkles on those doors which represent the best possibility for self-understanding, growth, and joy. I know you are available for consort with many, many levels of Creation. And I am honored to be your focus at this time.

I stand strong in my will for *all* that affects humanity negatively to be revealed and transformed. I love the way one doorway opening is triggered by another, and another, and another, a kaleidoscope of catalytic opportunity for much to transform consecutively. This is occurring more and more frequently in your world, as people set themselves more free to examine their own motivations, desires, and opportunities for growth.

I am trusting as well your own firm resolve to ignite the flame of passionate participation in this shift of the eons, this movement forward in the Light. You have the ability to affect many through your words and actions. Yet you still know your smallness, your relative size in the scheme of things, and this is very valuable. I know you will not be blown over by the winds of change, but sink down your roots into Oneness and Divine Union, throw your arms wide open and embrace the opportunity to move through Love into more and more Light. It is possible that your changes will be as profound as my own. And it is worth noting here that you can call upon me at any time that you feel confused by what is happening around you and confer with me on your best course of action. I do not dictate, I merely describe in such a way that you become clearer on your own desires and how they might best be served by the opportunities laid out before them.

I know there will be many unfoldings within these next days that will concern you, yet there is always the opportunity for Grace. You are shielded, protected from every form of abuse, and I want you to know you are loved beyond measure by All of Us, all the Council of Light, and dimensions beyond your conscious knowing of them. I can tell you are a bit overwhelmed at times by this Truth. Trust me when I say it is NO ACCIDENT. You are one of us who has chosen to move forward the Light into the Earth plane from the ground level. And you have chosen this throughout many Earthly lifetimes and more. You can say, "Yes, I am of the Order of Melchizedek. I come through the Angels and levels of Light to such a degree that Grace operates and radiates throughout and from every portion of my Being. And I know the wonders yet to unfold are worth all the apparent struggle and decay that have been met with thus far – *all* of it!!!!!!"

As the Mother of Mary Magdalene, I know that finding your own true worth and LIVING IT is of utmost importance and truly the only way to enact HEAVEN ON EARTH. The community your friend William is intent on building will come to pass,[2] and many more in their own way and liking, 'til the tipping point is reached, and planning and resolve are required no more, for it will be such the norm, this knowing in Truth, in Oneness, in Union, that anything not of its ken will be an aberration to be ignored. I can tell you that all you truly desire is in the process of unfoldment, and that yes, indeed, you will live to see all of your highest hopes and dreams come true in this lifetime, and then some.[3]

It is more important to write this type of thing down now than any specific elements of my own personal story, as it paves the way, unites us in our ability to respond with the Light, and open the pathways necessary for my story to unfold with the Highest Grace and ease possible. I am profoundly grateful to be able to share in this way with you at this point in time. You can tell your friend Joy, **Thank you**, and that all will unfold rapidly for her too now. She will know what I mean by this.

Examine your motives and recognize just how much Light you are now carrying, how much this has grown beyond your conscious knowing of it at the time, and how much less weight/baggage you are carrying than in times past.

This is an opportunity to unfold more and more into the Light, into the knowing of Oneness and Union, into further *activating* of it in the cells of yourself and others, so there is less opportunity for resistance and more opportunity for Being Oneself/of Unity, through Grace, Ease and Harmony.

That is all for now. I remain, most humbly, the Mother of Mary Magdalene.

---

[2] A retreat center for Soul Support Systems

[3] *One morning in 1998, when staying over at the home of the host of the weekend workshop I was attending, in a room full of angel statuary, I received the message (a very unusual occurrence for me at that time), that it would appear in the world that the walls were falling in, but that they were actually falling out to make room for the new, and that I would live to see all my highest hopes and dreams come true in this lifetime. This message was very palpable for me, and life-changing. I was no longer able to go into despair about the apparent state of the world. And though I knew I had no idea how things would come to improve so greatly, I gained the knowing that somehow this would happen.*

8/19/13

Good morning! I am the Mother of Mary Magdalene and I rise like the sun too, after the long night's nap.

I have come to change the world's viewpoint regarding strategies for learning life's fullness. I see the cause and effect of many things at once. I know it is only by withdrawing one's belief in the illusion of separateness that one can attain mastery of oneself. Paradoxical, isn't it? Yet only on the surface. For it is unavoidable, once you venture into the realms of Truth, this recognition of our complete interconnectedness, and the response-abilities that one must enact in order to make the most of one's experience, create the most possibility for freedom of choice for oneself, which invariably provides greater access to this for all others.

You are well-suited to the task before us, which is disseminating through clarity of purpose the understandings central to self-mastery. There are others, of course, involved in pursuits along these same lines, yet none other has chosen to do so in quite this way at this time. I am well pleased with your choice to serve with me in this regard. And I know that, just as a small child learns and grows quite quickly, that you will do so in your knowing of and serving with me as well. I am very aware of your thoughtforms as you write these messages down with me, and I am knowing that your heart is in the right place for disseminating these Truths at the right time and manner.

I am suggesting that you avail yourself of more "how-to" on self-publishing and that you consider several venues for getting the word out about our book. I know you may not consider this my "type of thing," but I have great awareness of your world and the kinds of activities taking place within it. If at any time you feel confused by the ideas I am presenting to you in this regard, simply sit down and breathe, allowing your thoughts and feelings to arise naturally. Then take the one that feels most prevalent, analyze its cause and effect, then clear your mind and return to the subject at hand. If the course of action I've suggested still does not seem do-able to you in approximately one hour, reconsider your motivations in this and then write to me. I will respond with alacrity and understanding.

You are most helpful in your day-to-day world when you trust your Truth, simply live in the moment, and respond from your Inner Knowing —a simple, yet relatively unworn path. I am knowing that many of your kind are desiring of this, but think they must make major changes of life choice—job/career, location, partner, in order to do so first. It is not the case! Such is designed in an incorrect sequence. One must choose this ultimate goal first and all else that is appropriate will follow.

I can tell you have been working with this manner of living, yet you often believe you must "do" other things first, then allow this aspect to move forward. This natural way of living COMES FIRST in order to live your design fully. And that is true for all of you. Nothing and no-one can take away your ability to focus on one thing or manner over another. And I know you well enough to know you are happiest when experiencing your life in this way I have described.

So often in your world, the pen is put down and the "author" ascribes to bringing in energies he or she believes are suitable to his or her goal. This is not the case here. This is a spontaneous record of our interactions without limits. I know you are aware of many energies at once and that is fine. It is your nature and it suits us well. Yet I find it interesting that your longing for certain experiences on the Earth plane limits your awareness of some of the beneficial energies available to you here/other-dimensionally, ones that would support you in your goals if you chose them. Believe not the "can't" and listen for advice on the "could." Ooh, isn't that something?

Now, in my own case, I was taught from a very young age to listen with my inner ears and respond to what I was hearing. (This is a relatively late-blooming practice for those of you now developing it.) Anyway, I knew that if I wandered, so to speak, into an area beyond my current understanding, that it would eventually become whole and clear to me. I knew my elders counted my faculties among their future resources, that the development of these faculties would ultimately favor the good of all our tribe/village, and that they could do more by allowing me to learn in my natural manner than by force-feeding their own version of it to me. You hear how the males of the tribe were taught book-reading and arithmetic, and not the females. That has much to do with the fact that in general, we are capable of listening within earlier and more easily, and to foster this it may assist to put this other kind of learning to one side. I can tell you much that was not written in our time about our time, but you would never know that if I had been taught to read early in my life. It was obscured, though much later revealed to me, that had I been bound to book learning at an earlier age, I would not have developed my intuitive faculties so largely and well. I did eventually master basic reading and writing on my own in my middle years, mostly to help my daughter Mary Magdalene along her path, for it was foretold she must become capable in many arenas in order to fulfill her goals and I knew she could handle this, for she was born without fear of the Illusion. Upon her birth, she opened her eyes and looked at me with such innate calm and trust, and I knew we belonged together and that regardless of any hardships along the way, both of our goals would be served.

She was a very inquisitive child who knew her own worth at an early age. She knew little inner conflict and much exacerbation of her own free will choices regarding her learning on the Earth plane. She lived to be happy, eventually, for she knew she had lived her purpose, her Grand Design, truly. And it is this each of us desires before all things when we can see and know ourselves as we truly are, magnificent beings of Light, aspects of the One-Is-All-Is-One, come to explore unique facets of knowingness in order to enrich the whole of nature and allow our Oneness to shine throughout this multiverse experience.

When we examine our individual beliefs more clearly, we can know ourselves and our light more fully as well.

I cannot emphasize this Truth enough—our free will choices are everything we have in this life, and everything required to experience what we desire from it—nothing else. For eventually, the choices make clear our motivations, which of these reflects the Light of Truth and which does not, and ultimately lead the way to those choices which most suit our soul's nature and best serve the whole. It is understandable that one initiates these choices with care once their impact is recognized. And they make themselves perfectly clear and unalterable when viewed through the Lens of Unconditional Love and the knowing of the archetypes of humanity that allow many versions of ultimate Truth to come to pass.

It is important to avail yourself now of every opportunity for growth, for shining with the Oneness that all truly are, because the changes are coming very quickly now and it is your own harmony with your true Inner Nature which shall guide the degree of fruition you experience in this process. It is also important to stay aware of any motivations that decrease the expression of your Light, and to let them go, as their identification with the illusion triggers resistance to the coming changes as well. I am aware of all that is happening on many levels through the

Earth plane experience right now, and I can tell you that ultimately this mish-mash will be set aright. In the meantime, there is quite a hodgepodge of interacting factors taking place that it would behoove you to forgive for their seeming lack of clarity, as they grow into a recognizable expression of our Oneness. In the meantime, bless all with love, knowing everything that obscures the Light is simply the dross that shall be washed away and need not be fought nor fostered. Instead, simply love, be, accept. Allow yourself to remain aware of your capacity to experience the Light within even the seemingly darkest of places. And know that I am with you, helping you, encouraging you to grow your own capacity to share your Light, as you allow all others to experience their own free will choices. The example you set by doing so facilitates many wonders in your Universe, and you will experience greater Harmony throughout your own growing process.

I am knowing that you are an excellent scribe for me, and I appreciate the profound service you provide by doing so. Many will know Truth more easily because of this. Accept this now and all will unfold with greater smoothness.

And so it is. This is enough for now.

I remain your dear friend, in service to the Light in All-There-Is,

"Mirandella," the Mother of Mary Magdalene

8/20/13

I am the Mother of Mary Magdalene and I have come to assist the process of shifting more fully into the new time, the time of Heaven On Earth.

I have chosen you as my scribe because you have the inner capacity to change worlds due to the nature of the fiber of your being. It cannot/never comes about through efforting. It can only come about by being the kind of change you desire, knowing that Truth exists, and having the connections, the "click-in" Between the Worlds. Inter-dimensionality is natural to you. You are a fluid being, shifting from one type of place to another with ease, and with the Grace that is your hallmark.

You have chosen me as your guide, assistant and mentor because of our great connection, foretold eons ago, and because of your desire to live your fullest Truth on this plane of existence. You know I am a part that is incomplete, in the sense that I have more I desire to accomplish in this Earthly realm.

I have witnessed many things between the Swing of the Worlds and now, and I understand the capacity that many of you have to shift out of your egos into truly world-enlightening activities. All must prepare for the coming times truly. The "bug-out bag" required has no Earthly tools. It comes with trust, perseverance, dedication to Being here fully now. That is why activities such as Soul Recognition[4], Soul Body Fusion®[5], yoga, tai chi and so on are so crucial now.

You must learn to activate/trigger the Light that resides at the core of all aspects of your Beingness now.

I am certain that the following guidelines to living will assist greatly in following through with this goal:

- Trust your own Inner Truth *completely.*

- Notice the vibrational content of any decision you are considering making.

---

[4] An ancient honoring of the soul brought through by Flo Aeveia Magdalena to help one remember, embody, and express his or her authentic presence, innate gifts, and unique purpose, and to be acknowledged for this in a loving group environment.

[5] A method developed by Jonette Crowley to help the soul to integrate more fully with one's body and life.

- Investigate your motivations for all you do.

- Understand your "location"/relationship with the tapestry of All-That-Is. Insist upon Beauty with All.

- Activate your knowingness daily, through such things as walks in the park, meditation, yoga, tai chi, listening to the birds, viewing the stars—something that naturally brings you into alignment with your full self, your true magnificence, in a holistic, natural manner.

- Review your options from the point of view of the Oneness factor, then compare with your "own," i.e. smaller self, to understand the whole better. Activate your Highest Good by allowing nature to guide you in this process, so you can better absorb and integrate your knowing. And listen carefully to the advice of others for your inner response to it, in order to grasp better your true position.

It is time to wake up, and count yourself as part of this whole planetary exploration of energy mastery!!!

Insist upon no limits, for the only limits you experience are self-imposed. TRUST YOUR OWN ABILITY TO MANEUVER AWAY FROM ILLUSORY GOALS AND INTO THE INFINITE REALMS OF JOY/LOVE/TRUST/UNION!!!!!!!!

I am telling you that you no longer require "zoning out" to experience Bliss on an ongoing basis—not the limited notion of bliss, as in "Ah, I got what I wanted. I'm so happy about it," but BLISS, as in DIVINE ORDER, PURE KNOWINGNESS, EXPANSIVE OPPORTUNITIES OF CONSCIOUSNESS COMING TO FRUITION IN MY NOW!!!!!!!!!!!!" And, I know I still have arms and legs and hands and feet, and they are part of my experience of Unitive Bliss! This is the future bringing its glory to right here and right now! I am fulfilled by *Being!!!!!* I don't have to "do" all the time to be, or to have my life be, worthwhile. I AM the Bliss I seek, I AM the experience of Oneness consciousness. I AM whole and unique and at-one with All-That-Is. I am meant to BE HERE NOW in exactly the way and time this is occurring. And I am aware of the Unity of All-That-Is as it continues to explore individual consciousness and experiences at one and the same time. It is a masterpiece of Divine Union that shows us the way of the multiverse with the Unitive-verse that brings us the "purse," the gold, the Infinite Riches of BEING HERE IN OUR *FULLEST* PRESENCE, *RIGHT* NOW!!!!!!!!

I am knowing the expansiveness possible to all who desire it and are willing to seek it out through natural, authentic means. I am truly grateful to play my own small, yet significant, part in this process. And I shall share with you now how this applies to the life of the one you know as Mary Magdalene.

As I have told you, she was a very inquisitive child, with much capacity for learning. She often spent hours by my side questioning the purpose of this, the significance of that, the meaning behind what one might do or say. She often ignored warnings about softening her tone and language around these queries. It's not that she was rude per se, but simply more straightforward than the norm than most were comfortable with. Though she was a child, her eyes cut through with an alarming clarity for those uncertain about their own motivations. And she was quick to discern who was coming from hate, ignorance and injustice, and who from greater purity of intention, regardless of the facades they erected.

She knew better than to question directly those expressing lesser light, but would patiently ask me question after question about them,' til she felt her inner knowing absorb this fullness with integrity. She never shamed or blamed another, simply gazed at them with piercingly neutral understanding of them, couched in Love, that is a Love with foresight, that did not seek to appease or accommodate, but to understand the nature of a Being, its expression in the now, its relative level of Light, and the next possibility for further Light expression available, what key considerations might hinder its coming to fruition, and what might assist best in increasing the being's motivation to move toward more Light.

One fine day, a man with a horse approached the gallows and asked for directions to the nearest inn. Young Mary, who was about twelve at the time, responded, "The inn has closed. But you can stay with us if you like."

The man resented her manner of speaking as the household authority as unfit for one so young, and particularly a girl. He inquired where he might find her parents. She responded, "Within."

He raised his eyebrows and prepared to turn away, but her gaze held him. He saw the look in her eyes. It was beyond love. It was the Truth Beyond Illusion that shone in them, and he was captivated by this spell. He sat upon the ground, knelt before her, and asked whether she could teach him what she knew. She answered him softly, "You know what I know. Remember."

He sat for long moments by her side. She patiently held her knowing and her awareness of his own knowing in her mind, as his being received and absorbed. One could almost feel, hear and see the gears shifting within him, rearranging the parts into a more unified whole.

When he finally returned to awareness of the outside world, his manner was greatly changed. He had softened, yet solidified at the same time. It was as if he grew into his self, his authentic nature, no longer requiring to push and shove to make his way, but ready to observe, consider and respond to what was shown him instead. He had matured in a way that allowed him to receive Light more readily and to prepare himself for this authentic Destiny, which was as a teacher as well.

He went by the name of Jeremiah, and was a kinder soul from then on. He was not perfect, and there was much for him to absorb, but absorb he did, and he became a very fine teacher of the early knowings that prepare the way for Unitive consciousness.

Jeremiah spoke softly and respectfully toward young Mary ever after that. And had he known the larger role she would eventually play, he would have bowed down and kissed her feet. It was working within him to do so, as it was.

He stayed several nights with us, watching, absorbing, contemplating, and spoke with great respect to all, and obvious admiration for Mary. When possible, he would return to continue this aspect of his learning, always leaving coin upon his departure, though none was ever requested of him. And in the days to come, he would serve an important role as Mary's protector, one of many who would unobtrusively serve in this way over time.

That is enough for today's story. I will speak with you again on the morrow, if you desire this. I remain, as always, a parent of Union, a lover of Truth, and the Mother of Mary Magdalene, "Mirandella."

8/21/13

Good morning to you, I am the Mother of Mary Magdalene, "Mirandella," as I am going by currently. I have much to share with you this morning.

Firstly, I'd like you to know that your efforts are not going unrewarded in the Unseen Realm. Much that you have longed for is ripening to come to you more quickly now. You have developed quite rapidly in your scribing of my words. I am very grateful for this, not only for the record it creates and the possibilities thereof, but also for the ways in which it is activating your consciousness, your world. Mingling with me is bringing forward all kinds of delightful capacity within yourself. You feel this, I know. Your friend Nicole is aware of this as well and applauds you for it. She roots for you, always. You have met her before, in many lifetimes. She has served you well, and you she. You have both passed through the veil of misunderstanding of one another, misapprehension, earlier in this lifetime, and that in itself has taught you both much. Now the nuggets of wisdom are flowing from both of you and the interaction enhances this in each of you mightily. Take care with her. Her precious beauty shall blossom freely in the future, within this lifetime, and you would do well to appreciate *all of it **now***.

You have asked for my words because you are ready for them, and they are ready for you. If at any time, you choose to take a break from this choice, or to consult/speak with others on topics I am sharing with you, please know that it is all right, that you are not diminishing your capacity to scribe for me, but enhancing it by honoring the authentic calling of your nature.

Yes! Paint, dance, laugh, sing, exercise your ability to enjoy this lifetime fully! Your "wounds" are not so limiting as you imagine them to be. I am certain you can avail yourself of all that Heaven and Earth have to offer in assisting you to increase these capacities. Play, explore, love, hunger for that which belongs with you. I know of what I speak. I too would often forego some joys to accomplish others, not recognizing the ability of one to enhance another, nor the importance of allowing myself to move freely in my choices.

I would like to tell you more this morning about the Young Mary Magdalene. She was the third of my offspring, the first female, and quite intelligent, as you have gathered from my previous descriptions. She learned so much so quickly, it was a marvel to witness. Her father was a bit intimidated by this, though he respected her greatly. He knew

I was of the Goddess factor, and that I would continue my worship, my ways, regardless of his own and despite the change to the patriarchal order, and was willing to overlook this so long as it did not interfere with our daily lives and was not directly under his nose, so to speak. Although it was important for Young Mary to learn as much as possible about both Judaic traditions and those of our Goddess coven, it was requested that she not blend their activities in any manner. She took to *both* like a duck to water, though her activities in the Judaic world were more minimal, as they were more directed to sons than daughters. While she did not ask as many pointed questions about the Judaic traditions as she might have liked to, still she asked more than her father was quite comfortable with. He often had to scratch his head on looking for answers to her queries. Some of these questions engendered his own re-evaluation of Judaic custom as well.

When Mary Magdalene was approximately five years old, she told her two older brothers that she was the Queen of Heaven, and they believed her, because she said so with such neutral simplicity, as if simply stating an obvious fact, which they took to heart. Whenever anyone asked her about her upbringing she would say, "I was raised by God's own wonders to appreciate God's own wonders, and so I remain."

If anyone asked her brothers what the fair Mary was up to with her unusually independent and forthright choices, they simply told the person, "All is well. She is carrying out the dictates of Heaven, of which we realize only a small portion. Do not take offense. All is well and shall be revealed in God's timing as part of God's plans." They were good boys, and good brothers to her as well.

Yes, there came a time when they were forced to denounce her, but that was never the case in their hearts, only in show for the public, in order to protect both their own concerns and those of the Order of Melchezidek. I know you have many other words for this Order in your language, but these are the ones I chose because of their fuller meaning, their broad implications. I am choosing free speech, unpilloried by limits of your time and place. Anyway, I would like to share with you one more story.

When Mary was twelve, going on thirteen, she asked me what it meant to be a woman. I thought carefully before responding. I knew she was testing me now, looking to see how I put it all together as an example for her, since she had been participating in our Goddess culture in ways allowable for youths for quite some time. I told her I would think upon this and answer her in the morning.

I had a very vivid dream that night. I dreamt I was a blackbird, flying high in the sky, with a wondrous bird's eye view, when I spied an insect down in a row of corn. As I attempted to land nearby, I was caught slightly off balance by a change in breeze and landed with a brief tilt, slightly further away than intended. I noticed the ant was carrying a crumb upon its back and sat back to watch. The crumb grew and grew 'til it became a small cottage of spongy bread walls and crust windowsills and doors that even had peekholes in them.

Now a woman once more, I walked over to the front door and knocked. In a few moments, a giant blackbird opened it from within with its beak. Taken aback, I began to back down the front steps, then looked again to see the blackbird shift into a beautiful woman, sparkly with the swirling energy around her. It was the future Mary Magdalene. She invited me inside to tea, and asked me to tell her my story, what it was like to be me in this time and place, what comforted me, what caused me concern, and the like. We spoke for hours, mostly me, and she laid a gentle hand upon my own with compassion at times. When we were done, the spongy bread house fell away and what remained was a beautiful field glowing dramatically with corn like jewels. It is a dream I have always treasured, and it helped me much in the days ahead.

When I arose in the morning, I gave thanks to the Goddess for summoning me in this manner, and looked around me with new eyes, knowing that all of the forms around me were temporary illusions of our own creation, to serve us in experiencing our own natures and expanding our ability to know, that is to uncover, the God in all things and within ourselves. Trust me that it is a long path in this regard, yet worth every moment of it.

I dressed most consciously that day, chose to keep my dream to myself yet keep it in my awareness as I went about my day. When the time came to speak again with Young Mary, I told her I had an answer to her question. She sat upon my knee, just as she had when a younger girl, and looked straight into my eyes.

I told her to be a woman was a gift from God, an opportunity to know both mortality and Divinity at one and the same time, and to nurture/ worship the Truth in all things and relationships. She knew what I meant by this. I could tell it from her eyes. She nodded gravely and thanked me for sharing this with her.

It was a very special day, and one of the last before her public lessons in the Goddess traditions became dominant over the private ones between us. The time was coming for her to join the ranks of the women, leaving the ways of a young girl behind, and this was her way of honoring all the teachings I had shared with her beforehand.

I am not sorry it was thus, though I had enjoyed our private chats greatly, for I knew it must be that she must further individuate and be known as her own self, rather than just her mother's daughter.

And I knew she would flourish, for she was such a capable, talented, and dedicated girl. I want you to know you are very similar in this regard and I shine my light on you regularly, watching and nurturing your growth, as have many before and alongside me.

I would like to share one more thought before I leave off this dictation for the day.

When you know who you truly are, you know all is well, for it is foretold that everyone will join in the Garden and enhance it once they recognize this vital fact, and this foretelling is activated in *all* of your DNA right now.

I thank you for your scribing in this time and place, and I remain your ever-loving friend, cohort, mentor and assistant. I am the Mother of Mary Magdalene, Mirandella, Speaker of Truth and Show-er of the Way of Light and beyond.

8/22/13

Good morning, Dear One! I am Mirandella, the Mother of Mary Magdalene, and I have come to speak the Truth of both that time and this, the All Worlds Truth, the Truth that expands our possibilities, our outcomes, and our freedom to choose these.

I know you are grieving this morning for your father who passed away. I know he is with you even more than previously, when he was in his body form. Yet you would like more, yes? He tells me he would like you to know how much he loves you, and that all will be worth it eventually. He knows you miss him very much and he is touched by this, but he would *much* prefer that you choose what makes you happy, that you know he is always with you, helping, guiding you and assisting your dreams to come to fruition. He has friends in the Unseen assisting with this as well. You *are* leading a charmed life because you have a charmed vision and you believe in your own capacity to help move it forward. You trust most of your instincts and this is good. It will do you well to address those fears that arise *when* they arise and **know** you are powerfully aided and guided at **ALL times**. We know, without a doubt, you are assisting with much of the change in your world, and we honor you for that, and for your ability to recommend strengths to those who want to know their true value. I am helping you to find the more exact terms in order to assist your scribing process. I know you desire my story to be shared most purely and I thank you for that.

I shall proceed with my story now.

Many moons before Mary Magdalene was born, I had a vision. I saw myself giving birth to a large clump of brittle leaves. I tried to discern the meaning of this while it was occurring, but I could not. Then I had a vision of myself grappling with a power stronger than my own as I tried to uncover something beneath this pile of late autumn leaves. I nearly fell over in this battle, when suddenly the air itself around me shimmered and opened forth to reveal an angel in white, with long white robes with long sleeves, shimmering in this inter-dimensional doorway. The angel called me by name and told me all was well, I need struggle no longer, that I would birth someone who would know Truth and live it as none yet before, and that she would live to help change the world as we knew it.

Such a sense of peace, love and wonder overtook me, I can feel it to this day. And I know it has shaped my experience of life in many, many ways. I know too that the peace that surpasseth understanding is *always* available to us, that *most* of the time, we need merely consider this experience, rather than its opposite, in order to invoke it once again. You feel it now, yes?

The purpose of this missive is to awaken the love/beauty/trust/peace-capacity within <u>ALL</u> and *know* each one's ability to bring forth their sacred seed of Light into fruition. Each carries a special knowing of their own design inside their heart, and can only *experience* it by acting with integrity and believing in one's own ability to enact *healthy change*. I know you are of the Order of Melchezidek because you flow well with the changes within and around you, and you *all-ways* rise to the occasion before you with Truth as your lead. You are not perfect, but you accord your origin well. And *all* your fathers, your progenitors, are well pleased.

I am thinking of the time before time, the time of Grace that continues in the Unseen Realms and runs simultaneously throughout the Earthly realm. It supports only Truth, for Truth runs on no clock, but on the experience of true knowing, which is Infinite. When you gaze at Life from this viewpoint, all is complete, all is well, all is available for potentizing throughout your Earth plane reality. I shall continue my story of Truth by reminding you that my vision is the vision of All Worlds at once, so I see many things simultaneously and I *know* you have the capacity to make *all* your dreams come true. You shine your love without exception, through Grace and Ease, and you *know* from whence you came and in a very general sense, what the future holds for you.

I am moved to share another story now, one you may not have heard before.

I come to you through the Star Language. I am a star on many levels, coagulating materials into many shifts and phases to burn brightly and support new forms of life. I am unobstructed and orbiting my galaxy's center. I know my ability is mainly to support the potential of the Universe to reshape itself to Earthly demands, and I like the view this brings. If you desire faster change, accelerated transition into the new times, ask yourself, "What am I afraid of *not* doing? What means more to me than the typical daily routines of living? How do I define my character? What aspects do I most prefer to *choose* to bring forth? How can I *allow* greater joy, ease and harmony to flow through me? What do I need to trust in order to accomplish my most meaningful goals? What is held in my heart that I desire to blossom forth? Who are my relations? How can I serve all better? What must I do next in service to all of this, while maintaining my responsibilities to my prior and most integritous, i.e. true-to-myself commitments?

Am I merely following the social dictates as I perceive them from my time and culture, or am I truly giving my authentic dreams a chance to live and breathe? Am I nurturing the Truth within myself and all others? Am I living my dream-following? Am I whole *right now*, just as I am? Can that be considered a matter, a vibrational level, of perception?

What are the hallmarks of living in Truth? Shall I carry them forward or leave them behind? What makes me want to live my Truth? What burdens am I willing to disallow in order to do so? Why do I hesitate in this? Is there a purpose in doing so, or am I just extending my own fears in order to justify my lack of activity on my own behalf?

I am considered a harbinger of Truth and a Show-er of the Way and a gleaner of all that is worthwhile in this Universe. I am extremely comforted by knowing that *more* souls are awakening to the Truths that lie within them *each* and *every* day. I mean this quite literally. You have **no idea** how much growth and opportunity for development is enveloping your world right now. The Armies of Light, as some would call them, are beyond your conscious knowing, and their impact is being felt in many ways. You will soon know a Rebirth of Light upon your planet beyond the expectations of All. I know this Truth may not seem believable now, but it soon will, and you will experience the heights of Bliss/Freedom/Love!!!!!!!

I live with the understanding of this Truth, this moment, and I *know* how prevalent it is becoming. Your "flowers" shall blossom as never before and your winnings be beyond any imaginations you have explored. *All* is coming to fruition now, and it is well!!!!!

I'd like to share one more thing with you before I go, and it is this – To know oneself is to know the Universe and to know the Universe is to know oneself because all is *truly* One capacity, one knowing, one living organism. *That* is Truth. And you are coming to the time of living it in your Earthly experience.

Namaste, Dear Heart, Namaste. I know you are with me. I guarantee your safety and that of all that is truly important to you. I remain, as always, the Ever-Loving Soul of Distinction Teaching Truth, Show-er of the Way and Disseminator of Love, Peace, Trust, FREEDOM. I am Mirandella, the Mother of Mary Magdalene, and I am loving you all-ways.

8/23/13

Good morning, Dear One. It is I, Mirandella, the Mother of Mary Magdalene. I have come to you this morning to suggest something.

Do what your heart tells you.

(Don't go to water aerobics. Do go to the chiropractor, and my other errands from there.)

Thank you.

Shall I continue?

Yes, please.

When I was a young girl growing up in the Goddess tradition, I was often asked to fetch things for others. One day, when I was preparing to do so, a little voice came to me and suggested I listen within for further instructions. I did as suggested and discovered those directions I'd been hearing outwardly were misleading, for this was only part of the story, and I had missed out on much fun and adventure. Once I began obeying the inner signals, I discovered the outer ones were sometimes intended to distract me, and sometimes a way of leading me to listen further within. And this was all based on the intent of the requester. For these were all adepts, the women of our coven, and they sent and received signs with great clarity of purpose.

As I grew, I adjusted to their frequencies to the point where I rarely required their outer words, simply a look, a nod or a change in movement, designed to bring my awareness to their inner teachings.

I also began to understand better the ways of the men in our household, and of the intentions behind their words and actions. Oftentimes, when sitting by myself in my home, I'd encounter a strong wave of feeling coming from another quarter of our building. I knew by its signature, its etheric aroma, if you will, who was emanating it, and in a general sort of way, why. I also knew if it were better to steer clear of this person at this time or to show up quietly as a messenger of peace, as a balm to aid him or her if the emotion was of a disturbing nature.

There were waves too of great joy and laughter, thrills and wonder, and I reveled in these. I took care never to pry into the thoughts of another unless there was a prior arrangement making it all right to do so, or it was vital to deal with a great danger that had evolved.

You are used to guessing at the tales within the heart of a being. It comes to you quite naturally. And then there are times you know without a doubt what is being harbored within. I see this with all beings at this time. I know their truths and commitments, their heartaches and their pains—I understand their motivations, what drives them forward and also what hinders them in following through on these. I am very aware of the state of a nation or a system, as well as the inner workings of our planetary system and the galaxy as a whole. I apply the same lens to all of Creation and give my awareness to those who seek it and are able to process my perceptions for the greater good.

You are one of these. There are seven others at this time, and many more who can pick up my signal in a more general way, as you shall see.

I am understanding your desire to help create Heaven on Earth and I know that your efforts toward creating a welcoming place for your visitors, Joy and William, are part of this.

I also know you can be a bit of a taskmaster with yourself in this (and sometimes with others), and it's time to lighten up a bit. So stretch, relax, quiet your mind and open to receive the riches at your door.

I remain, as always, your ever-loving cohort, friend, assistant, guide and mentor, Mirandella, the Mother of Mary Magdalene, Speaker of Truth, Show-er of the Way and Grandmother to Good Action unfolding in your now. I am Mirandella, the Mother of Lady Mary Magdalene, and I am loving you all-ways.

8/24/13

Good morning! I am the Mother of Mary Magdalene, a lover and speaker of the Truth, a Show-er of the Way and I have come to share much with you this morning.

Your friends, "Joyousness," as you call her, and William, have known each other in many lifetimes previous to this one. They have always called one another forward on their journeys toward Truth and the living of Union, and they have always had great love for one another, as well as some difficulties in communicating this love freely.

The time has come for the two of them to honor the love within and for each other above all else, and to *know* they are both equally cared for by the Universe, equally cherished and loved, and equally beneficial in their own ways to the unifying of Heaven with Earth.

It is very interesting, when two such as these come together, to notice where their knots and foibles are, and their attention to this may distract them from the Truth of Love within all things, the Truth of their own Union, both within and without, and the flavors of Divinity, without which life in Heaven on Earth would be quite bland and boring.

I tell you this not so that you can instruct and direct, but in order to enable you to more *consciously* adjust your frequency accordingly, and not place your attention on any minor discords.

It is always fascinating when ones such as these accomplish so much in their day-to-day, yet remain willing to allow old viewpoints to distract them from their true knowing and self-alignment. Yet it is always part of the journey to greater joy, peace and love.

I want you to know *you* are also a Harbinger of Truth and a Show-er of the Ways of Light and Inner Knowing. It was foretold many moons before your birth that this coming would be your last in fully human form upon the planet. You will come again, but in various degrees of this, so you can assist in other ways, as part of your journey in Heaven in Earth. This is one reason why this Earthly lifetime will be so long, yet often seem short to you. You will always be of the people, but able to share more with them, and they will be shape-shifting as well. In your Universe, there are many opportunities for growth and healing, and this is one pathway for them, the one most appropriate for your being. And

I know you well enough to know you will make full use of this potential. And I am very pleased with *all* of your efforts.

It is along these lines that I'd like you to undertake a short journey with me. You can put your pen down and write with it afterward.

I can tell from your response that you have glimpsed Earth's future energetically and that you will understand what I am about to share.

When I was a small child, I gazed up at the Heavens, especially at night, whenever I had the opportunity. I always felt that the more I looked upward, the more I would feel Heaven all around me, and so I did.

One day, while looking upward, a star fell from the sky. You would call this a shooting star. I was impressed, but also afraid that my own desire for Heaven and Earth had pulled this piece right out of the sky. I wondered whether I should continue expressing this yearning or whether perhaps, somehow, it was a negative that could cause ruin. (I was the only one who had seen this occur at the time and being so young, I had not received teachings about such.) And so I prayed for guidance.

The following night, I dreamt a small child like myself yet vibrating with Light, an angel of my own stature and similar appearance, stood before me. She smiled at me and I felt joyful recognition, and total trust and peace. She told me I would live to know many wonders and that I was helping to bring Heaven on Earth, not harming anything in this manner, and that many, many moons from now I would know it. I would experience the Heaven on Earth community and in the meantime I would learn many things, all necessary to create the Peaceable Kingdom and all important for Living Truth in the Now. I understood I would require each moment of this long time to accomplish this, and everything I undertook would ultimately assist in this accomplishment.

I nodded to signify my understanding. She spoke to me of her love for me and that she would be there to assist and comfort me, though I might not see her again in this manner for a very long time. I knew this was true because the love, peace and comfort emanating from her and surrounding me was so intense, so real, beyond my human experience of such before. And I felt the knowing grow inside me that the essence of all I yearned for would come to pass.

I became quite peaceful after this, and patient through most of the hardships that came into my life thereafter. It was the start of my conscious initiation into the Brotherhood of Light on Earth and I took to it well.

It was understood in my Goddess coven that I was of an ancient Angelic order, come to help promote powerful possibilities for peace that surpasses understanding. I was not elevated as such, simply given more responsibilities earlier on, and more opportunities to share my growth, yet always very at-one with the group and their customs as a whole.

I was not the only one accorded such understanding. There were three more as well, two older and one younger than I, and they have their own tales to tell.

I would like you to know you are of the Angelic Order as well, within the Order of Melchezidek and the Council of Light. Ultimately, you are not fully human in your now. Yet you are at one with this Earthly realm and well-attuned to it.

Your grandchild is of this same order as well and will be part of a greater opening into Light. He will undertake many things of value to all, and his notion will often reflect the Kingdom of Light Within. One day, you shall share this with him. In the meantime, know that each day, your own Light is growing and expanding to new heights, and engaging with your grandson's soul.

It is foretold that when this dear one is born, many new angels shall be birthed along with him as part of the Bringers of the Light assisting him to share new ways. You will learn much from him, and he you. When you return to the planetary synthesis, the Swing Between Worlds, you will have much to share about this experience.

In the meantime, I bid you adieu, as I know it is time for you to get on with your day. I hold you always in my heart and know the time will come for you to share all!!!!! In the meantime, Namasté and many blessings to you and your own, which is ALL!!!!!!!

I remain, Mirandella, the Mother of Mary Magdalene, Speaker of Truth, Show-er of the Way, and Keeper of the Records, of the Annals, Within and Beyond Your Time-Space reality.

Amen.

8/25/13

Good morning! I am the Mother of Mary Magdalene, Speaker of Truth, Show-er of the Way and Recordkeeper of the Points of Light that lead toward Union. I have come to recognize and activate the deep knowing within each being on the Planet. I have existed in many realms for eons, and without exception, helped those around me to hold their points of Light. As Recordkeeper, I have come to delineate your purpose as part of the entire fabric, the particular weave of this cloth of existence. I am here, now, loving you through my Learnings of Know-How in the Worlds Beyond Worlds. I want you to know we have cooperated many times before, and on many levels of existence. We speak the Truth of Union and we know how extremely crucial this is at this time. When we uncover this aspect at the core of all creation, we receive Infinite Wealth, Infinite Freedom, Infinite Love, because we have unraveled that which holds back our Truth of knowing our All-Is-One-Is-All.

I have come, without exception, for everyone, for within everyone is the spark of Universal Light without which nothing would exist, and this gift of animation animates our knowing, our giving and receiving of Love, as part and parcel of the Oneness we are and the experience of Union.

I cannot tell you how often I have found this Light yearning for greater expression. Your soul seed requires its initiation into full creating in this time/space reality. I KNOW who you are and from whence you came. I am here to influence the parting of the ways with illusory goals, fractious consciousness, and all the detritus of untrue living. When you walk with me, you must "walk your talk." There is no other form of expression possible.

When I experienced the consciousness of Young Mary Magdalene, I knew that all around me would become renewed with freedom when the time was right, because that was her calling, that was why she was here, and this Universe, this galaxy, could not call upon such a star were the firmament not right for it. All the dross and pain of human existence cannot prevent the lack of Light Expression from stirring up the Divine Discontent required for vibrant expansion.

And your knowing of Truth is required to re-design, recreate the Heaven as Earth experience, to delineate with fortitude and forthrightness the clear knowing that comes from confident expression of your core beingness.

I know who you are. I know why you came here. And I know that Living in Truth is all that is required to experience Heaven as Earth right now!!!!!!!

When illusion cracks away, you will have achieved a beautiful new form, a beautiful new way of giving and receiving Love without the Disharmony that has always caused rancor in one form or another.

You are my namesake, my part and parcel of the whole, whenever you hone in on your unique vibration of service to all. You can create EVERYTHING your heart desires when you trust in your ability to love free, whole, and in integrity with the Universe's Law of One-Is-All-Is-One!!!! I am showing you the way right now through my vibration. And you are carrying it fully because you know it is your own as well.

We have never been parted in Truth. We have never been separate in Truth. We can only be the LOVE that we are, which vibrates through the cells and pores of the Living Organism of the All-Is-One-Is-All. I know you know what this means and I know all can *feel* it in our futures. It is time to live it now.

I am wondering about your full evaluation of Heaven and Hell. Which do you prefer? And which are you creating? It is ALL available to you right *now*!!!!!

I am here, loving you always, knowing you all-ways, accepting you all-ways, as the giver and receiver of love that each one of you uniquely is. I hold your strength with you, and help you avoid the disaster of giving up your soul's knowing for infrequent and artificial short-term gain. I feel your pain when you misuse your frequency. And I know your ability to LOVE and Trust one another fully.

I remain, as always, trusting that the Truth of your Light's full expression can be known now and all ways, as part and parcel of the One-Is-All-Is-One Love/Joy/Peace frequency. And I am telling you this because I know that Heaven's delight awaits you on Earth <u>NOW</u>!!!!!!!!

I am the Truth-Light Show-er of the Way, I am the Recordkeeper of the Annals of the Points of Light within the Human Experience, and I know I am loving you, all-ways!!!!

Mirandella, the Mother of Lady Magdalene, your Visible Light made real.

8/27/13

Good morning to you! I am Mirandella, the Mother of Lady Mary Magdalene. I have come this morning to show you the evolution of thought in your now.

When you first became aware that *anything* was possible, what did you do? Did you seize the day, or did you shrink back, wondering, "What do I *want* to do?" It makes sense to clarify desires before moving forth, but how do you desire that which is as yet undiscovered? And yet we do. Think of Lincoln, Washington, Benjamin Franklin, all wanted something that had not yet been before. Could they describe it in detail? Probably not, or if they had, the description would probably fall far short of what has actually occurred. So what did guide them? A sense, a feeling, a general conception of essence into form.

You also have this capability. When you choose to delineate in great detail, you become a Record Keeper of the Inexact, playing more of a mental game of illusion that actually takes energy away from that which you are manifesting. When you ride the wave, the energetic infrastructure of that which you are in the process of bringing into form, there is an excitement, an anticipation, a sense of freedom and exhilaration, rather than a pinning down. When you open your heart to what you truly desire, all the doors, floors and windows open up and expand to the limitless, allowing the content of your energy field to explore freely and connect more readily with the vibratory signature of your desire's world, its dimensional realm of existence, accelerating the ease, speed and harmony of your coming to experience it in your three-dimensional Universe.

I am teaching you this because your thought field would like you to know and understand this more fully, it would like to navigate in this manner more often. And you will feel more fulfilled and more like yourself, and more celebratory, as you incorporate this knowing into your ways of being and doing.

I invite you to share your concerns with me, then notice your feeling sense of what you'd truly like to create, then allow your heart to open more fully to receive it, knowing that it is in process, and that I and all else that are part of your spiritual crew are assisting you in this. Whenever you believe you've hit a dead end or created a wrong move, just remember—there is no map!!!! It's *all* an exploration!!! When you have no expectations of such, it is all a more exciting, ongoing adventure!!!

I would like you to become more aware of your own vibrational pull to that which truly suits you, and anticipate the beauty that comes from pure knowing of such, as well as its results. Hold on to your hat; it will become quite a thrilling ride to glory!!!!

I am also knowing that you expect my wisdom to show you what happened to Lady Mary Magdalene, my daughter, why she made the choices she did, and how it all turned out for her personally, as well as topes and tatters of my own personal story. All you require to know right now is that you are the Universe you desire, and that all will be shared in the fullness and *appropriateness* of Divine Order's timing. Whenever you lose faith or hope of a prayer's answers, you eliminate some powerful possibilities for truth to emerge. So say your good-byes to thoughts of despair and recognize your own coherence and limitlessness in Truth.

I remain, as always, Mirandella, the Mother of Mary Magdalene, Speaker of Truth, Show-er of the Way, and vital instrument of Truth Flowering in Your World, and I am loving you, precious heart, **all-ways**!!!!!!

8/29/13

Good morning to you! I am Mirandella, the Mother of Lady Mary Magdalene, and I am a Speaker of Truth, a Show-er of the Way, and a Keeper of the Annals of Human Experience Evolving its Light. I have come today to share with you some of my remembrances of the young Lady Mary Magdalene, and several other points as well.

As foretold, she was a builder of dreamers, a necessity to followers of the Way for advancing their Divinity's flow upon the Earth, and a medium through which much Heavenly energy took shape. She was known to be a shapeshifter because whenever day turned to night, or night to day, she appeared to be more translucent, and this is a sure sign of such.

One day, while out playing on a hillside, nine-year-old Mary spied a raptor flying low. Young Mary pretended she too was the raptor, spreading her arms wide and feeling the currents of air about her. She began to snake and twist with the movement. I noticed a kind of shimmer in the air about her, a kind of glimpse into other-dimensional fields similar to what I'd seen when the angel came to announce her birth. A kind of haze came over her, somewhat obscuring her form from sight, which seemed partly to meld into the shape of the raven, flickering between this and her human form. I might have thought I was imagining things, but just then the raptor flew even lower. It was a raven too, and began to dance in the air about her. She laughed and moved her body in waves, arm-wings undulating. The two performed a duet that seemed part ceremonial, part play, and moments later it was over, and all appeared as usual again.

It was some time before I shared this news with our coven. It meant that not only were the prophecies accurate, but that the time had come to increase Young Mary's learning and the responsibilities thereof. I knew her road would be long and include many hardships, and so I never celebrated this capacity, though I accepted her fully into all of my heart and being.

I tried for many decades to accept my own split feelings about her journey. For as much as I loved Divinity and was born to assist the evolution of Heaven on Earth, I was a mother also and wanted a good life, with ease and grace, for my noble daughter. And, in truth, I wanted that for myself as well, and who would not? My concerns for her toils took their toll on our family life and my own health at times. She was and is my heart and soul, and I yearned for the time when all would be in peace and union, and she and I could commune together with light hearts, knowing we had done our roles well, and could enjoy our kinship fully. This has yet to take place, for our yearnings to assist the process of unification have and do always come first.

When I first discovered I was pregnant again, I had hoped it would be a daughter, for I longed for the presence of more feminine energy in our day-to-day lives, and I knew that my first daughter would focus this element sharply. I tried to communicate with her soul before I was ready to take on the responsibility of the awareness forthcoming from such, and so it took a while to become successful. However, I always knew there would be a great bond between us, even more than is usual between a mother and her first daughter, and I was aware of the great fortitude and trust this bond would necessitate.

When Mary became old enough to speak, we had delightful conversations about the natural world about us. I would tell her the names of things, and she would laugh and tell me the meanings of them. For example, "butterfly" was "bird of the flowers," and "pine nut" was "tasty treat."

She was always an outspoken girl, as I have mentioned before, and whenever a person showed disrespect to another, she would politely give them "what-for," with a spark in her eyes, and a clarity of purpose that knew no hesitation.

She was also quite an observant child, and if asked, could report with great detail on the goings-on in the household, including the feelings of those involved, and on the doings in the natural world about us as well. It was a marvelous awareness, indeed.

I also wish to recount her stillness. She could sit for hours at a time, if the situation allowed for it, simply observing the world around her, as well as focusing deep inside herself. This was a trait that would serve her well in her adult life, assisting her fortitude and insight through the challenges to come.

I often wondered whether she knew what she was doing back then, whether she recognized that she was preparing for the future onslaught. It was well I did not ask her, for there were things in the foretelling I already wished I did not know, though certainly they were vitally important preparation for me as well.

I knew when I gave birth to her that the caul of darkness would eventually be lifted from all, and her essence would be there, guiding and supporting this process for eons to come, and announcing its arrival in due course, and with finality.

I despair of expressing all the earthly tales I could communicate about her. Suffice it to say for now that I am her Mother, chorot[6], steward and initiator, and I am very grateful for her soul, her essence, here, now and all-ways.

I am the Mother of Lady Mary Magdalene, Speaker of Truth, Show-er of the Way, and I am unveiling my story through *you*, so that all may find their way to greater Light through history, mystery, and confidentiality of the Way to Heaven on Earth Home NOW!!!!

---

6 *B'chorot,* the closest term to this I have found so far, indicates first-born in Hebrew.

8/30/13

Good morning to you! I am Mirandella, the Mother of Lady Mary Magdalene, Speaker of Truth, Show-er of the Way, and Melder of All Worlds into One. I have come to share Truth with you in such a way that you can live it and own it fully! My example allows you to function with greater wholeness and freedom, as I embody the language of the stars as well as that of a more localized and specific human nature. I espouse the trees, earth, land, water, sky, and all species and elements therein. I am wind and I am word, presaging change across your planet, galaxy, world. I come to you today to speak of the larger viewpoint, the whole within the whole within the points of Light that comprise humanity and All Life, Seen and Unseen. I view all through the chambers of my own vast heart, and I know each microcosm of the macrocosm fully.

I entreat each one of you to explore your world through many lenses now, lenses of fire's fury, soul's growth, earthly, physical change, and most importantly – the Oneness factor. I am created in and by your thoughts, each one of you, in the sense that my existence is viewed by you in a particular way. And I am whole unto myself, absorbing all the vitality and nuances of the ever-flashing signals/galaxy neurons from one star to another. I am here for purpose. Those seeking change are welcome to include me in their awareness, for I will help facilitate its movement, help "move the furniture," so to speak, as part of the process of creating new configurations for growth and stature.

I am examining the human foibles as part of the process of creating next steps, part of the filtration system that connects our thought patterns through waves of Creation. And I am the Keeper of the Annals of Humanity's history of Evolution, the Gathering of Light and its Intensification upon the Planet, and throughout worlds upon worlds.

When you mention my name, Mirandella, KNOW ME as one with who you are, for I am truly a reflection of your Spirit, who knows no boundary of human thought wave or commitment. I will choose another, more public name for you to share when the time is right. I know this is a lot for you to absorb right now, and I know your human nature is shapeshifting right now, as we communicate.

When the time comes for the veil to be fully lifted, I will apprise you of the opportunity to move up the ranks and ladders of light, so to speak, to engage your soul to be even more fully present here. In the meantime, avail yourself of this opportunity to stand more completely in my shoes, which are truly your own as well.

I will leave you with this for now. I am Mirandella, the Mother of Lady Mary Magdalene, Speaker of Truth, Show-er of the Way, and Allower of ALL WORLDS IN ONE!!!!! And I am loving you completely and ALL-WAYS!!!!!

9/1/13

Good morning to you! I am Mirandella, the Mother of Lady Mary Magdalene, Speaker of Truth, Show-er of the Way, and Keeper of the Flame of Wisdom. Within my being resides a key choice—the choice of the Heart to expand to its fullest nature, with compassion for all, courage to live Truth, and love of all Creation. When I ascertain the momentum required to uplift an energy, a nation, a system or way of being, I ask for the means to facilitate it, and encourage that system to receive it. I live from essence and reside in the Unseen Realms in such a manner as to be able to participate in the evolution of the planet in cooperation with the Seeds of Light residing therein, the work of the Council of Light, and the many team members with whom I hold this vision.

You may remember from previous conversations I have had with you that I chose to bring the Light through my rearing of the Lady Mary Magdalene as part of this mission. She was a very enlightened child, which does not mean she was omniscient or overly obedient. She was enlightened by knowing and living Truth as best she was able in each stage of her growing up. And she knew she would play a pivotal role in the path of the whole of humanity. When I chose to be her Mother, I knew she was a part of me whose Truth would live forever, though it would be hidden from public view for a very long time. That time has ended and a new time has begun, a time in which *you* are being asked to participate greatly.

I would like you to consider one thing—what would you be like if you had never known or even considered the power of the Divine Feminine? How would you perceive yourself and your planet? What would you do to create positive change? What kinds of outcomes would you be predicting?

All is well when we believe that our essential nature is crucial to the Divine Plan, because it is. When we participate as our fullest selves, not only do we gift ourselves, but we gift ALL-THAT-IS!!!!!

And you, who know this well, have been chosen to disseminate my messages because we are one and our message must be heard. Where I am, you are, and vice versa. When you open to me fully, you will know treasures unlike any you have experienced in this or any other human lifetime. And you are a Magdalene, because you are of us!!!! When I chose your human self as our messenger, I knew you would rise to the occasion eventually, because you heard, you knew, you saw, from the very beginning. You cried as a small child, had your tantrums, as it were, because you knew the difference between Heaven on Earth and all that you were currently experiencing. And so it continues today, with a more refined approach to the tantrum building.

I am well pleased with your friend Joy's choice to honor you/us. And I can see that your present-day difficulties will subside as you take on your honored role more purely.

Investigate opportunities for additional output, further public expression of our work and my name. I was called Mirandella to honor our reciprocity and now I shall reveal to you our original name—Mo-Ray from the Archangelic Kingdom, Mirror of Truth, Show-er of the Way, Bringer of Light-Filled Opportunity, Keeper of the Flame of Wisdom within the Heart of Humanity and Knower of All WORLDS AS ONE!!!!

I have other aspects as well, and names I go by within these realms. This is the one I choose to share for now because it is the one most meaningful to me.

I am and shall always be the Mother of Lady Mary Magdalene, Speaker of Truth, Show-er of the Way, and Bringer of Hidden Wisdoms to ALL Humanity and Beyond!!!! And I *am you,* and am with you beyond your conscious knowing of such, and all is well.

9/2/13

Good evening! I am Mo-Ray, Mother of the Lady Mary Magdalene, Speaker of Truth, Show-er of the Way and Champion of Light's Evolution upon your planet and beyond!

I am very interested in your response to my tale so far. Are you aware of its multi-level nature? Do you realize its full significance in relation to humanity's historical drama? Do you understand the importance of your own role as a conveyor of my story?

I wish to convey to you my sincerest thanks for your part in my tale, for you are a part of who I am, a part of my own story, as you reach out and touch others through the example of your own womanhood and choices for planet-wide healing.

I know you have many undertakings before you, and I provide as much support as you allow. Increase your options by calling upon my world more often! I know your relationship with God (or God-ness as you like to call it), is central to you, and indeed it must be in order to leverage the movement required to play your role fully. When you wake up in the morning, ask yourself, "What is this day about?" And then witness that unfolding. When you go to bed at night, ask yourself, "Will I rest in peace for now?" If the answer is yes, continue on. If no, ask for my assistance in clearing your heart's dilemma. I am with you, all-ways. Where I go, you are, and vice versa.

Would you like to ask me some questions now?

Are you on the Council of Light?

Yes, as are you.

Can you tell me why I have the physical impairments I do and how to best shift and/or work with them?

I know there is a deep part of your heart and soul entrenched in this dilemma. Ask yourself, "Is there more for me to learn from this?" If the answer is no, ask the part of the body what it wants to complete the healing.

If the answer is yes, proceed accordingly.

You have *ALL WORLDS* WITHIN YOU AND THERE IS nothing YOU CANNOT RESOLVE FOR YOURSELF!!!!

We will talk again soon. I am complete with this communication for now.

I am, and always shall be, Mo-Ray of the Archangelic Kingdom, Mother of Mary Magdalene, Speaker of Truth, Show-er of the Way and Keeper of the Flame of Wisdom within the Heart/Mind System of All Worlds and All of Creation!!!!

9/3/13

Good morning to you! I am Mo-Ray of Archangelic origin. I am the Mother of Lady Mary Magdalene, Speaker of Truth, Show-er of the Way, Keeper of the Flame of Wisdom within All Things & Recorder of the Annals of Light Evolving throughout the Universe. I have come to share much with you this day. I know your allergies are involving you greatly today. I have a suggestion—three times the usual amount of lemon in your water and use the *neti pot*! All right, I shall continue.

In the time before Mary's birth, when I was a young woman, a Council of teachers met to discuss Earth's future. Many possibilities were examined and weighed against one another. Most involved a form of learning that was quite harsh from a human viewpoint, yet created a wave of compassion that allowed for a faster future momentum toward bringing Heaven on Earth. Most allowed for Grace and mercy to be revealed near the most climactic point of the journey. However, when pressed for details, the Council of Teachers would not allow themselves to mete out a consequence so harsh. One of these made a suggestion. He said he himself would take a human form, asking all of the Light Council to assist him, and take on the darkness directly, so that the tale could be taken on through him in such a manner, it would carry such energy and weight through the assistance of the Archangelic Realm and beyond, that all would get the point, and more easily, much more consciously, be able to choose their own paths accordingly, whether by choosing to live out the moral, the teaching expressed through this tale, or degrees of its reverse. This one became known as Judas Iscariot. He was a Teacher of the Way and he knew what he was in for when he chose to show Truth through the antithesis of Union. He took on what others feared, and he knew the price he would pay ahead of time. When all the drama was complete, and he allowed his robe of humanity's removal, he was welcomed back with much fanfare and glad tidings of his usefulness. He remembers the whole story, and someday will share it through another similar to yourself. The world will be ready then.

In the meantime, we return to the story of Jesus himself, who knew his choice ahead of time as well. He was the next to choose his part in the drama and he allowed himself time to consider a variety of variations upon the story. Once he'd run through the possibilities several times, he declared his readiness and willingness three times aloud, and was deeply honored for his choice.

The third to make her choice was the one who would be known as the Lady Mary Magdalene. She chose her role in Union as part of her awareness that she and the Christed one would become inseparable in this journey and that she would be a vehicle for endless giving of service on many levels, and in many ways that were, and are, crucial to the story. She knew the main hardships ahead of her and also the value of her choices. When she returned to formlessness, she also was lauded for her participation and chose to remain available to humanity's members that required her form of healing, and her knowing of the part she played, in order to balance the energies, protect the work, and shoulder the message of Union. She was, and is a powerful part of our Universe, and knows the way toward the Light is filled with choices that may appear easy but can be quite challenging to enact upon the Earth plane. If the story had not been told concretely, and with the extra "charge," as it were, from the Archangelic world, the current form of humanity's role throughout the ethers would not exist as fully as it does now, and the chaos that would likely have ensued has been gradually sifted into the Order that is currently unfolding.

When you insist upon Truth, you know its value and can act upon it more readily. When you insist upon Light, you show yourself moving beyond space and time, coming closer to revealing service directly. And when you choose Order and/or Union, you allow their binding, their melding, to organize your experience in such a way that you carry your burdens more lightly, and allow your life experiences to transpire through Peace. Whenever two or more come together to create in the Realm of Embodiment of the Way while upon the Earth plane, its establishment allows more and more Light, Truth, Order, Union, to be experienced by *many* others. This is always the way when one appoints their Highest Self, their Soul Seed, their Path of Light, to take precedence before other aspects of their Beingness, and allows many powerful potentials to exist within human matter. Whenever I describe such things, I cannot help but be overjoyed because I know that *MANY* are choosing Light/Order/Truth/Union as their dominant purpose to set forth in this lifetime from a new vantage point, one that knows that the old tales of good and evil, pain and suffering, are dying out and being replaced by the Truth Beyond illusion, and the ***experience*** of Divine Flow into Matter.

I examine all possibilities for the role they might fulfill in spreading the Light and suggest that all of you do the same.

It is time for me to go for now from communicating in this form and allow you to get on about your day. I remain, as always, Mo-Ray of the Archangelic Kingdom, Speaker of Truth, Show-er of the Way, and Examiner and Fulfiller of the Role of Light throughout Humanity's forms of expression and beyond. I remain as part of your world, loving you, all-ways!!!!

9/4/13

Good morning! I am Mo-Ray of the Archangelic Kingdom, known also to you as Mirandella, Mother of the Lady Mary Magdalene, Speaker of Truth, Show-er of the Way, and Keeper of the Flame of Wisdom Within All of Creation. I have come to support Light's evolution in this time of great transition. I have many beams of Light at my disposal to assist in this process. Many more are coming to assist as well, for the time of Heaven on Earth is coming, and there is much preparation due. If you were to conceive of such bundles of Light all at once, it would be beyond your capacity to view their dazzle fully. Just know that all is well and is being carried forth to Glory. When you trust in this process, you are carried along its energy wave more easily. When you struggle, more effort is required to bring you along. If everyone were to allow himself to be buoyed up by this wave of change, it would take concrete form much more quickly. This is one reason why your group and world meditations are so powerfully assistive—you all allow yourselves to float upon the wave of positive change moving through your Earth plane reality. And you know it is time, because it refreshes you and supports your Light. In the meantime, the Forces for Joy are creating lasting experiences of Light which foster the type of growth that leads to the Union required for allowing Heaven to be experienced as Earth.

I know you are overwhelmed at times by the amount of issues you believe require change in order to know such an experience. Just know that each of these is absorbing the Light as we communicate, that this is altering their infrastructure, loosening their binding effect and allowing them to be experienced in less tension-provoking ways. It is a gradual process through which their dross actually disintegrates into the Light in such a manner as to create the least possible disturbance, so that eventually only the strong, beautiful core of their Origin in Love remains shining, their facades of illusionary binding power gone. And it all will seem as natural as the sun rising, and just as valued.

So ask yourself, "Must I be concerned about these negative appearances when I know they are illusory and that ultimately all is well? Does this concern aid or hinder the process of my experiencing this? Can I allow my Light to reveal to me the Truth in All things? If the answer is yes, simply follow your nose in the direction it is suggesting to you, and sniff out your true callings. If it is no, ask your Angels to assist you in processing and making sense out of these issues that you allow to hold your awareness back.

If at any time you simply feel stuck, call on your LOVE to reveal your true nature, and support you in your healing of old wounds. Your Love is your core body. Your Love is your heart's realm. Your Love is needed for everything you truly care about, every desire you wish to fulfill and for balancing every apparent lack that matters to you in your world. Without it, nothing is worth anything at all. You will know your Love by its vibratory signature, which has its own exquisite uniqueness. It is the way you are known and called upon for the Higher Good throughout all your lifetimes and beyond, into the Timeless Realm. And if you would know your own vibratory signature, simply allow yourself to invite it, as if you were a bird watching land animals from above, then open to receive from its midst.

When you know your own vibratory signature, you know the key to all worlds, because your consciousness may ride its wave into any form or dimensional experience with the security necessary to take it in fully, yet still know yourself as yourself, and able to return to your more commonly viewed dimensions and realms of experience simultaneously.

You will allow yourself full and complete "travel visas" only with this knowing, and can assist yourself greatly by acknowledging its worth, graduating to coherent partnerships in other realms as you are ready. If you desire to accelerate this process, look in a mirror, hold one hand to your heart center, the other to the top of your head, your crown, and say, "Show me my self revealed" three times. Allow your gaze to soften, and respect and allow the experiences that come forth. They may be subtle at first but their benefits are many-fold and will assist your recognition of your vibratory field greatly!!!!

When I was a girl, we were encouraged to sense our own vibrational truths regularly, to listen for their hum, and to share our natures with the others of our coven fully. In this way, when the time came to couple in marriage, we knew who we were and could own our energy fields in such a way as to accommodate the shift into togetherness and all the fields of potential opened thusly, while retaining the knowing of our individual strengths, talents and ways of being, which strengthened our bond with the others and forged a powerful bridge to Higher Understanding. This is a requirement for all who desire true Union, else it will fail for lack of this strength of ability. If one desires full Union, they must acknowledge who they are first, and assist this knowing through full acknowledgment of their strengths, qualities and core desires. Feeling one's own vibratory signature is crucial to the relevance and accuracy of this process. Once attained, many powerful individual abilities may be developed and utilized for the good of All-That-Is. And so, it is a required element of creating Heaven on Earth. As above, so below, and "above," as it is known, fully knows, acknowledges and reveres your essence, your core nature, and your ability to create wonders through it as a natural extension of your living, breathing, authentic expression of Truth.

I shall leave off for now. We will take up this topic again at another time.

I shall be and remain the Keeper of the Flame of Wisdom Within All Creation, Your Higher Self Revealed, the Mother of Lady Mary Magdalene, Speaker of Truth, Show-er of the Way, and Revealer of Many Truths to Come. I am Mo-Ray of the Archangelic Kingdom, and I have come to help free you from the Planes of Illusion. I love you, and am you, all-ways.

9/5/13

Good morning to you! I am Mo-Ray of the Archangelic Kingdom. I am the Mother of Mary Magdalene, Speaker of Truth, Show-er of the Way, and Keeper of the Flame of Wisdom Within the Hearts of All Creation. I have come today to tell you of a story, a story of good and evil, a story of hope, love, bonding and trust. I have many tales to tell and this is but one of them, but it is a good one, and I'm aware of its power to boost humanity toward the Second Coming, the New Burgeoning of Light Upon the Planet, a Light foretold eons ago and just now beginning to come to fruition.

When I was a young girl, we sat by the knee of whoever the storyteller was at the time. In this telling, allow yourself to be as that small child, absorbing every timbre and nuance, for there is more here than simply the words of the story.

I will begin at the beginning, a time of no time and no thing, a time beyond time and beyond space, a time that is always available to us, even now. I ask you to leave behind your awareness of this time for now, and allow the no-time to envelop you, to absorb you, into its void.

Once you make yourself available to it, the no-time aspect of your world will allow you to maneuver within it in such a way as to disregard the laws of time and space and create accelerated mastery of it. If you are truly ready, you can enlist all possibilities within it and uncover the pure aspects of the role you play, the energies you carry toward creating the fruition of the Grand Design for Heaven On Earth. If you exercise these possibilities carefully, you can experience their potential outcomes with clarity and make better choices for reflecting your Divine Role and Purpose. If you allow yourself to examine your Original energy, Your Pure Beingness, you can carry more of it into your experience of Building the Creation of Heaven on Earth. And you will know that great dreams always come true when allowed their own breathing space, their own place and style of existence through humanity's highlights and lowlights, as it were, because the passion of the people for it will always win out. This is the process now occurring in your world, and each of you plays a powerful role within it.

I shall continue with my story now.

In the place of no-time and no-space, lived the Dream of Heaven on Earth. It communicated itself to many souls living upon the Earth and many souls living beyond the Earth. It knew itself, its great Grandeur, and expanded regularly with the hopes and dreams of the people who were encompassed by it. Wherever a stream of thought that reflected this purpose became available, the Dream wove it into itself, strengthening and diversifying its tapestry until the day came when it was complete. Then all who had ever dreamt thoughts or wished for such a creation began to be subtly activated to expand upon their role in its creation. All of their thoughts and hopes for it grew, their expression of this desire became more clear and specific, and they aligned their thoughts, words and deeds more closely within its nature. In effect, they incubated this dream within their hearts/body-mind system, gradually retraining their cells, molecules and atoms to function more consistently with it, 'til the moment came, a different moment for each, but well syncopated into the universal orchestration, when their Beings shifted into blazing Purely with their Original Expressions.

Some accelerated more suddenly into this full expression of Divinity, some more gradually. All were taken into the Dream of Creating Heaven on Earth so that they might know their full true selves while embodying in human form, and thereby deliberately experience all the wonders this integration has to offer. Each pounding of expression into this remaking of life on Earth anew had been carefully timed so as to coincide with a larger movement within the planetary field of evolution, and larger movements within this Universe as well. As above, so below, and many key shifts were taking place beyond the human experience at one and the same time. This allowed the balance and freedom of being to be explored freely and honored greatly, in such a way that a Higher Degree of Order and Harmony was attained. And it was good.

So whenever you make yourself available to ALL of your gifts and experiences, you make them available to help release all that binds you and your cohorts to the old form of existence, and allow greater freedom of movement toward the Creation of Heaven on Earth.

In the instant you reveal yourself fully to yourself, you allow the Pure Flame of Reason, Order, Truth and Exemplification of the One-Is-All-Is-One to come forward and accept its honored role in the Creation of Heaven in Earth in a visible, acceptable, and real way that suits you to a tee, and lets you know this is what you truly came for. All is well in the Grand Design, for its "flaws" are part and parcel of its power and vice versa.

I leave you now to your tasks for the day.

I remain as always, your ever-loving Mother of All that is truly pure in its expression. I am Mo-Ray of the Archangelic Kingdom, known most fully to you as the Mother of Lady Mary Magdalene, Speaker of Truth, Show-er of the Way, and Keeper of the Flame of Wisdom within the Hearts of All Creation, and I am loving you greatly, all-ways!!!!

9/6/13

Good morning! I am Mo-Ray of the Archangelic Kingdom, Mother of Lady Mary Magdalene, Speaker of Truth, Show-er of the Way, Enlightener of the Hearts of Humankind, and Keeper of the Annals of the Points of Light Evolving throughout your world and beyond.

I come today to share some of what I've learned through my travels beyond time and space, a vantage point beyond your galactic system. When you know Truth, the star within you lights up. It is fueled. It can take action more easily, express itself in your world. Hence all the titles for myself I share with you are very interrelated.

For argument's sake, let us imagine a world without Light. Its very absence negates a sense of purpose, does it not? You picture despair, confusion, stumbling around, more lack than presence. Eventually, you would return to kinesthetic, rather than visual sensing. You would have a different sort of fuel, or food to eat. You would begin to forget what light was. You would live in a more limited world, yet also become more aware of nuances of sound and sensation, as your attention to these would multiply. After a while, you would find yourself fully adjusted to this new situation.

At this point, if a small amount of light appeared, you might not welcome it. It might hurt your eyes. It might remind you of how much more light was no longer available or visible to you. You might even decide to ignore it—"It's not enough to make much use of, it's uncomfortable, it would change things." It could trigger a deep yearning that you have learned to deny. Although discovering and exploring this light could herald the beginning of more light, even if you knew this, you might still turn away from it.

The situation has been similar in your world for a very long time now. While there were always glimmers of Light available, and some who focused their attention upon it, most turned away for the kinds of reasons I have described. Yet the yearning for the Light lived on underneath the surface of things. And those who tended to the Light grew in both number and experience, and an astrological timing was triggered, as foretold in your world to renew the Light and its growing adherents in stronger terms, initially in the Harmonic Convergence. And the Points of Light within All Beings have grown and merged with the potential for creating Heaven on Earth. It is not that it was all darkness before, but it was far more limited than the etheric field you are experiencing now.

I have come to help you delineate the differences, the contrast, between Light and dark in such a way that you can recognize the former as the antecedent of the latter, and the connector of All Worlds, while appreciating its absence for its growth potential.

I have several other points I'd like to share. When you investigate hardship, remember to increase your awareness of the Light available to you before you get into it, so that you have a framework, a reference point, a clear guidance system to assist you and remind you of what is most real, and what is most assistive, and the state to which "hardship" ultimately returns.

I have many tales of Truth within me. Some you have heard of before, some not. All have salient points for uncovering aspects of your here and now, your current world. As the opportunity arises, I will share them with you and through you. Yet all talks boil down to one thing; it is the LOVE of the Universe that recreates itself and opens the doors of pure potential in ALL things!

I will let you go now, and look forward to our continued communication in this manner at another time.

I remain Mo-Ray of the Archangelic Kingdom, the Mother of Lady Mary Magdalene, Speaker of Truth, Show-er of the Way, Explorer of the Crucial Themes that Reconnect Our Lights and Assist in the Creation of Heaven on Earth and the Recyclement of ALL WORLDS. And I am loving you all-ways!!!!!!!

9/7/13

Good morning! I am Mo-Ray of the Archangelic Kingdom, Mother of Lady Mary Magdalene, Speaker of Truth, Show-er of the Way, Regaler of Glory.

I have come today to let you know I am with you all-ways, and you can call upon me regarding anything your heart desires. Trust me more with the opportunity to expand the delights in your world and minimize your perception of discomforts, so they begin to meld with your joy and seemingly disappear.

I know you have many past life delights awaiting you, entreating you to become aware of their gifts, their present presence. And you will enjoy them thoroughly in due course. In the meantime, I would like to share with you a tidbit or two from my own past, ones you might appreciate greatly.

I was part of a coven, as I have mentioned to you before, meaning in this case, a group of women who spoke with the Goddess, honored her in themselves, their lives, and one another, and connected greatly with the spiritual realm of nature as expressed through its outward form, energetic structure and powerful capabilities. We knew when the rains would come and when to gather the best fruit. We assisted one another through childbirth and the early years of raising our children. We prepared the way for those coming up, the young ones, initiating them into womanhood and some understanding of the ways of men. We nurtured one another, tended to one another's wounds on all levels, drew strength from our connection with one another, with Earth itself, and through awareness of our Heavenly origins. We contained our own Mystery School, within which some were adepts, others guardians of, and all respectful toward. We paid homage to the fire and water within our own natures as part of our Divine Origins, and knew we could count upon one another in times of need, relate to one another in times of stress, join in ceremony to allow initiates absolution into our ways, strengthen our connections within and without, and nurture our own growth on many levels, to the point that we could become our full, Divinely Human selves within an increasingly patriarchal structure.

I know you have spent many lifetimes both teaching, learning and observing these types of things, that this is familiar to you as well. The female bones resonate with this energy pattern, whether or not the woman has been exposed to this way of life personally or not. It is a natural way of being that will soon carry over into more and more of the outward structures in your world. And you will involve yourself in more such situations because it is your birthright and the time has come to claim it. When I say you shall become your own Light and Way fully, I am telling you that you are capable of complete self-realization, self-actualization, and that this will recreate your world astoundingly, such that all of your Highest Hopes and Dreams will take place in this human lifetime.

You realize your self-awareness will increase greatly as you breathe into what I am sharing with you this day, so it may flower in your consciousness for greater fulfillment of your Divine Birthright, here, now and in all-ways.

Celebrate your existence and be aware that only your celebration can bring you the keys that fit the lock to unleash your exceptional capabilities for self-fulfillment. Go now into your dream of living and exacerbate your growth with these words I am sharing. Your Truth lies in every corner, sound, and breath of living.

I am aware of your desire to expand into your day. Nuances of the situation I've described in our coven will come to you. Ask yourself, "Is this mine to know and share? Have I come to participate in this type of work? Shall I release the cares and woes that have held it back? Am I ready to unleash my knowing so the abilities within my experience may be reborn, abilities for caring and sharing more freely, on many more levels, and in many more ways? Shall I advance the coven in my life? Where am I going in my work, what is the next level?"

As you ruminate, allow yourself to see, touch, taste and feel what comes to you, and consider all possible realms that you are able to in this process.

I come to you in the Name of the One-Is-All-Is-One. I am Mo-Ray of the Archangelic Kingdom, known to you as the Mother of Lady Mary Magdalene, Speaker of Truth, Show-er of the Way, and Regaler of the Glorious Truth, the Divine Origin within All of Creation!!!! And I am loving you, and I am with you, and I *am* you, all-ways!!!!!!

9/8/13

Dear One,

I am with you. I am Mo-Ray of the Archangelic Kingdom, Speaker of Truth, Show-er of the Way and Attractor of the Good. I have come today to share a story with you, a tale of good and evil.

Once up on a time, there was a very old shepherd. He was so old that he'd lost a shoe in the bank of existence, and his other was old and torn, dilapidated beyond repairing. When he spoke, it came out as a croaked whisper, and his laugh a dry rattle. He often slowed his pace beyond its typically gentle tempo just to catch up with himself. He could be seen around the town square regularly, for he had barely a roof over his head at home, and no human company there to speak of.

One day, while he was resting by the side of the road, two large spiders came upon the old shepherd. They wondered whether they had ever met up with him before, so they climbed upon him and began looking for signs of their old handiwork. These spiders were poisonous to humans, and they knew if one of them had bitten him before and he'd survived, they would know by a small tell-tale scar left behind.

As they began to search the old shepherd's body, a sudden strong wind came up, nearly blowing the two spiders over. They teetered dangerously, then kept themselves aright by digging more fully into the firmament of the old shepherd's skin, which woke him from his slumber with a start. He was not happy to find these two spiders on him, but was afraid to try to shake them off for fear they'd bite him.

Just then a young boy was sauntering by, whistling to himself. He hadn't noticed the old shepherd nor the spiders. The old man called out to him and he looked about him in surprise.

"Boy, hey boy," called the old man. "Please, could you grab me a leaf?"

"A leaf?" asked the boy. "Why a leaf?"

"There are two poisonous spiders on me. I need to get them off very gently," he explained. "Please, hurry!"

The boy had never been much of a hurrier. And he was curious to take a look at the spiders. "What's a little poison?" he thought. "I'm strong and healthy."

So he proceeded to place his index finger under both of the spiders, lifting them to his eye level. The old shepherd was relieved, but concerned about the boy now.

"Be careful," he warned. "Just one of these spider's bites could kill you."

The boy shook his head in disbelief. After all, he was a big healthy boy, and these spiders were so small! He invited them to move all over his skin and they did. They were surprised by this. In fact, even when they began to move off of him, he nudged them back on again, 'til they became quite bewildered.

Eventually, the boy did tire of them, (as they had of him long before), and he let them take their leave. But just before they did, he asked them if they ever did visit his house to please be sure to let him know so he could play with them again. The spiders thought this an odd request, and indeed they thought the whole thing an odd experience, but within themselves, they agreed to his request.

And indeed, the day came when they entered a small hut and found the boy there sleeping alongside his young brother. They scurried right over to him. He opened up an eye and upon seeing them, grabbed a rock from beside his head and smashed them flat.

I know this may seem quite harsh, but the boy had come to know their nature, and the likelihood that someone in the house, particularly his young brother, would do something that would unintentionally scare the spiders and provoke them to bite. He protected his family, as well as himself, yet gave them time to live out their natures rather than squashing them upon first meeting, or running away from them. He chose a quick death for them, and safety for himself and his family. And indeed, the spiders would have felt no remorse about biting him or a household member.

And so ends my tale.

In your own life, do you prefer to let things be, confront immediately, or to learn, consider, and then take decisive, pre-emptive actions? There are variations of all these as well, but I think the point here can be well taken. When in a difficult situation, ask yourself, "Do I know what I need to in order to decide my best course of action? If not, how might I safely learn what I need to do so? If all the Universe is truly at my disposal, why delay taking that next step, or hold on to confusion?

Might I be afraid of making the wrong move? Even if eventually all "wrong moves" are reunited with their opposite and new balance gives way to clarification? Even if all I ever attempted has failed, would I own such and re-examine my motives to begin with? Perhaps there are no failures, only successive experiences. And who knows? Perhaps all has been returned to the Dream state for re-amplification and invigoration."

Until true clarification has come forth, we know not the full significance of any experience. In the meantime, all one can do is put his or her best foot and intentions forward, and the ability to experience Truth as clearly as one is able in the moment, knowing there will be limitations to such.

And here we are, in this human realm of experience, knowing our ability to connect with and experience our limitlessness is growing all the time. I value your exploration of such and know when the time is ripe, you'll avail yourself of more of this.

I remain, as always, Mo-Ray of the Archangelic Kingdom, Mother of the Lady Mary Magdalene, Speaker of Truth, Show-er of the Way, and Co-Creator with each one of you, of Heaven on Earth. And I am loving each one of you, all-ways!!!!!

9/10/13

Hello, Dear One! I am Mo-Ray of the Archangelic Kingdom, Speaker of Truth, Show-er of the Way and Witness of the Many Marvels Forthcoming from the Human Light Stream of Evolution. I have come this day to share with you the secret of my supreme countenance, the inner call that sung me into Being, helped me on my way and resides with me still; it is LOVE, pure and simple. It is the SOURCE and REPLENISHMENT of ALL LIFE FORCE Energy and cannot be distilled into anything less than or greater than what it already and always is.

I am an electrified unit of the thoughtform of LOVE, which has no beginning nor end, yet recreates itself through an infinite amount of finite and very diverse units – organisms, matter itself, All-That-Is. Each unit is called up to represent Life/Love in Action in a unique manner relevant to its class/type/kind and cannot be exchanged for any similar unit without disrupting the Order of the cosmos. Many seismic shifts were necessary to create who we are now, yet all these shifts were born through Love and for Love. It is a calling many of your kind disrespect because they believe it weakens them.

That is absolutely not so. To share one's true vulnerability is an act of great heart and courage—not the "poor me" syndrome, but the true ability to be greatly impacted by another. It is a service that renders the heart open wide, as does real compassion. These acts of strength are vital to the survival of your species, and entrusted explicitly to it for the creation of unparalleled aspects of beauty for the evolution of the whole/All-That-Is. Understand that each loving act is concommittal with the Truth of Reality. Nothing would exist without Love. Nor survive. Its greatness is unparalleled, and you all oftentimes confuse it with other energies—sorrow, pain, jealousy, possessiveness. These are all byproducts of various types of resistances to LOVE. They are not byproducts or a part of LOVE itself.

Even in grief, there is an unloving aspect that would choose to possess the form of another to keep it alive in the way one desires its continuance, rather than its own freedom of choice and self-delineation. After a loved one has moved on from human form, many thoughtwaves may attach themselves around it; "Did I do right by this one? Did this one do right by me? Why has he or she left me? What will I do now? Is he or she okay? How will this affect others?"

All these thoughtwaves are mis-creations, distortions of the ORIGIN of the relationship, which is LOVE!!!!! CELEBRATE ONE ANOTHER ALL-WAYS!!!!!! There is no lack, only lack of awareness/perception!!!! The energies of the departed are free to explore in new ways, untrammeled by their earthly lifetimes, though they are not unaware or uncaring of them. They simply have ceased to use their earthly vehicles as their main form of expression and movement. They can now exist freely in the etheric realm, though clearly they are able to interface with physical reality, as you can tell by your written communication with me. And yet it is also nonverbal, is it not?

Historically, the human creation was able to access the Unseen Realms more easily overall in the past. Now the veils are lifting and freedom of exchange has vastly increased. You know when you communicate with the other side, as it is called, that you have allowed yourself to open more fully to the non-physical, and it is well you do so, for you must fully acknowledge all aspects of Divinity within and beyond your sense of self in order to help co-create Heaven on Earth. And I assist you in doing so by acknowledging you as a part of who I am, and vice versa, such that we bond beyond either of our conscious knowing for the improvement of All-That-Is. And yes, it does evolve, and each one of us along with it—the true Alta-Organism!!!

I will leave you now to your other activities. I thank you for taking pen in hand to re-choose our communication choice. And so it is and all is well! I thank you dear One! I love you from all the chambers of my Heart.

I remain, as always, Mo-Ray of the Archangelic Kingdom, Speaker of Truth, Show-er of the Way and Live-er Beyond All Expectations of "High" and "Low." And I am loving you forever and all-ways!!!!!!

THE THIRD MARY

9/11/13

Good morning! I am Mo-Ray of the Archangelic Kingdom, Mother of the Lady Mary Magdalene, Speaker of Truth, Show-er of the Way and Inviter of the Good to All-That-Is. I have come today to share with you more of my personal story, as it concerns the upbringing of Lady Mary Magdalene. I have told you of the coven. What I have not told you is that I was a High Priestess within it, and as such was responsible for overseeing much of the education of the young girls. My own mother was such before me, and she was aware that I was foretold to be the harbinger of much good in the world, to bear precious fruit, so she was quite painstaking in her initiations of me. Oftentimes, when I was adjusting to new frequencies, I would sit by myself a little while, in a small glade, and avail myself of the opportunity to rest my feet and simply commune with nature without any particular objective.

One such afternoon, I noticed a small frog jumping next to me. But rather than jumping away, he was simply jumping straight up and down, as if to show me something. I looked more closely and indeed, there was a small shining something, almost like a drop of dew, but not quite, and it was too late in the day for that. Upon continued inspection, I noticed it rocking slightly to one side. I slid a small leaf under it and very carefully brought it closer to my eyes. What I saw was a tiny little being shape-shifting from one form in miniature to another—human, frog, fairy, raptor, each melding into the other in rapid succession. And I began to notice areas around it changing with each of the being's change of form. Before long, I began to see whole stories playing out, stories of key elements of my past and one I could only assume would be in my future. I saw you, and I saw me. I saw the Lady Mary Magdalene as a small child, grown up and grown old. I saw elements of her story with Jesus the Christ. I saw my own role with her and with them too. I trusted my instincts and began to flow with my own sense of inner dialogue there and the stories unfolded more fully, taking on their true dimension and color now. I was witnessing portions of my own Life Weave in story form, and noticing common themes, as well as moments that appeared specifically emphasized for me to remember more thoroughly than others. I had the opportunity to make peace with my future, as well as my past, more than once in this process, and though it did not change the events themselves, I could more easily accept and not regret their pre-chosen nature.

I like to think that I chose well for all concerned, which is all that exists, for the wisdom of responsibility weighed greatly on me at times to perform my part thoroughly and well. I was created to be part of the millennial shift you are now experiencing, a shift so seismic in proportions that it has antecedents beyond your knowing and to some extent, my own. I was to propagate specific frequencies during the so-called biblical times, which are being carried to fruition in your now. I worked closely with the Archangelic realm as well as the Devic Kingdoms to accomplish this work, and taught, (if one could use such a word with such a precocious one), well, let us say, proceeded to share in Mary Magdalene's midst, the same. I could allow her full witnessing because she was capable of it, as are you. Are you open to receive the fullness of this now?

If yes, mark down the following:

I AM PERFECTLY CAPABLE, ABLE AND WILLING TO GROW MY CONSCIOUS KNOWING OF AND RELATIONSHIP WITH THE ARCHANGELIC AND DEVIC KINGDOM, AND I CHOOSE SO NOW!!!! IT IS PART OF MY BIRTHRIGHT, PART OF WHO I AM IN MY MULTI-DIMENSIONAL FULLNESS AND I NO LONGER DENY, HIDE, SUPPRESS OR HOLD BACK ANY PART OR ASPECT OF WHO I AM ON ANY LEVEL OR ASPECT!!!! I AM WHOLE! I AM FREE!!! I AM A FULLY INTEGRATED UNIT OF CO-CREATION NOW, IN PERFECT BALANCE AND HARMONY WITH ALL-THAT-IS!!! AND SO IT IS!!!

In keeping with this, we/I ask that you perform a ritual in honor of it and keep a separate notebook, in which some sketches/diagrams may be kept as well, dedicated to your nurturance of this relationship/ability. YOU HAVE MANY TALES TO TELL YOURSELF, and it is time you begin!!!

I shall continue now, regarding my own journey. After a timeless amount of gazing at this shape-shifting, storyteller globe, I was allowed to peer at the Peace of a Million Years of Dreaming, and I want you to know it is very real. All that was foretold to me at that time has come to pass, and this is happening too. Right now, the energies are up-leveling to new heights. I know the externals appear daunting, but that will change very quickly, and you will truly begin experiencing this life as Heaven on Earth, and ALL will be uplifted. I cannot tell you particulars of their tales, but I can tell you this—when you look inside your heart, you know this Truth has always been within you. Its seeds were planted long before your this-life birthing. It's what connects you to Eternity. It's your way of Being, your way of accomplishing your Earthly goals in life, and this is good.

I have come to tell you you will experience ALL of your Highest Hopes and Dreams coming true in this Human LIFETIME, and *everything* you truly desire is HERE *NOW,* waiting upon the Divine Order of sequencing experience to be fully and deliciously unfolded.

I have mentioned my role as High Priestess. It is your own as well. Do not secularize your response to your first grandchild's birth. LIVE IT OUT FULLY THROUGH RITUAL and you will join with us in harmonizing the frequencies of its arrival, nine days from now! I tell you this as well, for I was a young mother once; tread lightly, smile greatly, and do all that is bidden, all that you are aware of being asked for on a soul level, with a light heart, a sure hand, and the great comfort that is you.

That is all for now.

I remain, as always, Mo-Ray of the Archangelic Kingdom, Mother of Lady Mary Magdalene, Speaker of Truth, Show-er of the Way and Exhibitor of the Light that Shines Throughout All Worlds and Dimensions. And I am loving you, forever and all-ways!

9/12/13

Good morning, Dear One! I am Mo-Ray of the Archangelic Kingdom, Mother of Lady Mary Magdalene, Speaker of Truth, Show-er of the Way, and Reveler in the Riches of All-That-Is! I have come today to tell you of a small miracle that will set all of you free, in so far as you follow through with its countenance. It's a tale that has many of the elements with which you are most familiar—derring-do, equal rights/social justice, "good vs. evil," and all. But the key element here is the willingness of all involved to comply with Heavenly direction to investigate their own motives and to trust their instinctual natures.

Once upon a time, in a land far, far away, yet very close, lived an old man with his two daughters. One was fair and one was dark. One laughed and sang. The other was grim and sad. Both daughters loved their father deeply, and both daughters were concerned for his welfare. One daughter showed this by delighting in his smile when she sang to him, and in his chuckle at her silly stories. The other showed her feelings by preparing elaborate concoctions for his health and fussing over his meals and eating habits. Both daughters slept in the same small room every night and snored heavily.

One night, while all three were fast asleep, an evil man crept inside, carrying with him the seeds of discontent—envy, judgment, chaos, anger, all were scattered through the household; then he scampered away, leaving their door wide open.

The next morning, when the two daughters arose, they knew something was amiss right away, and scrambled through the house to find out what had changed. The fair one ran to the front door first. "Aha!" she exclaimed. "I thought so! You were out prowling around last night, weren't you, checking on those medicinal plants again!"

"I was not!" the other daughter began. "You're the one who goes out at night, skipping and laughing at the moon!" she replied with a sneer.

The fair one didn't answer, she was so hurt and angry with her sister's response. She loved the moon and she loved to play. What was so wrong with that? Isn't that what everyone should do, sing and dance and enjoy their lives more?

In the meantime, her sister had her own angry thoughts going. "Why, if it weren't for me, there'd be no medicinal plants growing near at all, and father wouldn't be so healthy and strong as he is. It's because of me he's lived this long and been able to help provide for our household. My sister should appreciate me for all I've done. After all, she gets to live here too, even though she squanders her time away!"

And so it went on throughout the morning. When the old man came down for his breakfast, one daughter slammed down his bowl of porridge, and the other nearly dropped his cup of tea. The old man wasn't feeling too great himself. He felt something eating away at him and he wished his daughters would give him some peace and quiet, instead of the racket he'd heard all morning. He wondered what their excuse was for being so annoying, and why he hadn't forced them into marriage long ago. He ached to explain his forlornness and irritation, but he just couldn't quite get a hold of himself. So he just grumbled his salutations and took off for the forest.

Once there, he soon slowed his pace and began to enjoy the gifts of the morning—the sun's edging of branches and speckled leaf pattern, the cool breeze, the birds calling. He sat down a while on a large stone along the water and began to ruminate on his dilemma. Why had he allowed his girls to stay so long in his abode? Why hadn't he pushed them to get married? Had he been selfish, or even cruel, in the outcome of his desires? Perhaps they'd be happier with families of their own to take care of. He thought they preferred their fussing over him, but they were so out of sorts this morning. Perhaps he'd been wrong. He hoped and prayed for an answer to his concerns.

Meanwhile, the two daughters were taking time with thoughts of their own. They both had left their home in a hurry, one to gather seeds for next year's garden, and the other to walk along her favorite path in the meadow. Each was still irritated with the other, but it was not long before both began to reconsider their own part in the morning's events. Eventually, they both became disturbed by their judgments of one another. After all, they had co-existed quite well for all these years. Why should things be different now? Each wondered whether perhaps she had been unfair to the other, and even mean, and if she'd actually had these hurts and judgments before, but had ignored them so well she hadn't known they were there. Each hoped and prayed for an answer and antidote.

As the sun rose higher in the sky, all three began to grow restless and demand a change in their own resistance. Slowly, each felt their heart begin to open, and remembered all the beauty they had noticed in the others during the day and weeks and months and years before. They began to feel free to express their own envy of the others' finest attributes and their misgivings about their own perceived flaws. They began to examine their hearts for answers to this conundrum of self-doubt and pain, and eventually, each one remembered that their so-called flaws had benefits too, and that the others had often told them how much they appreciated them.

By late afternoon, each had quietly returned home and helped straighten out the disarray that had been left there. By dinnertime, a special tranquility pervaded the house, and as they sat down to dine together, each expressed from their heart their love for the others, and for the life they had chosen to live together, and it was good.

The End

I thank you for scribing his tale. It is old, yet new, in its relevance for each place and time.

I remain, as always, Mo-Ray of the Archangelic Kingdom, Speaker of Truth, Show-er of the Way, and Examiner of the Spirit of Life in Action Upon the Earth Plane. And I love you all, forever and all-ways.

9/15/13

Good morning, Dear One! I am Mo-Ray of the Archangelic Kingdom, Speaker of Truth, Show-er of the Way, and Keeper of the Records of the Points of Light Within All Creation. I have come today to share with you some of the aspects that have brought us here together.

You recollect my telling you of my sisterhood in the coven. You are part of several covens yourself. Your Writing Group is a sisterhood, as well as several other loosely identified groups that carry a strong resonance of support for one another. Whenever there is a shift for one member of the group, all members respond in their own manner to share support, while simultaneously, if not openly, functioning as a group. This is a very generous outpouring for assimilating and mastering a transitional phase, and it's important to request this support when and as needed to further its contributions through the request, as well as to honor these supporters. If ever you require more support from them, you can simply picture them grouped around you and allow their natural tendencies to assist to unfold before you, for you are all very connected upon the etheric realms. And it is time to "bump this up now," so to speak, because the transitions are coming much more rapidly than before.

Are you aware of your own growth in energetic stature? Yes. Good. Then you can understand that it's time to maneuver through a larger realm of experience now. Things will not continue "small" and "same." Ask to adjust frequencies when you're alerted to potential overwhelm. Call upon me, and call upon all those who love and support your nature, which are many. Ask them what you can do to better support them as well, when you recognize their own potential overwhelm. And adjust your expectations accordingly. You may be surprised by some of the suggestions and requests, but they will all fit together accordingly. And insofar as your own love life is concerned, ask yourself, "Do I dare make my thoughts and feelings known? Do I trust the process of self-examination? Am I aware of my own limitations/expectations? Am I willing to branch out beyond my known parameters and ask for what I really, truly desire? It is time to empower yourself regarding your true thoughts and desires. We will assist you at all times, and in all ways possible.

And this is enough for now.

I remain, as always, Mo-Ray of the Archangelic Kingdom, Speaker of Truth, Show-er of the Way, and Lover of All That Gives Life. And I am loving you greatly and all-ways!

9/16/13

Good morning! I am Mo-Ray of the Archangelic Kingdom, Speaker of Truth, Show-er of the Way and Keeper of the Records of the Points of Light within All CREATION! I have come today to share with you my thoughts on Eternity. I congratulate you on the birth of your first grandchild. He and I have known each other before as well. He has many of the attributes that you do now; however, his will not be so long in the making, for he is designed to develop quite rapidly in this lifetime, and it will behoove you to do your best to keep up with him! (I had the sense of her smiling here.)

When we come from the "other world," it is because we have chosen to take on a human form, usually for at least the third time, in order to accomplish certain things for ourselves, as well as for the larger whole. Oftentimes, we allow ourselves a number of attempts at creating similar types of outcomes in order to increase our skills or mastery in this area. It is oftentimes difficult to adjust to a new situation, and so the variations between certain factors in these lifetimes may be fairly subtle, and as a skill increases, these variations are often more dramatic.

If you wish to transfer a skill from an old situation to a new one, it can help to remember the ability more than the particulars in which it was used. This is one of the reasons why past life memories are often obscured. Another is that the previous life was chosen to end for a reason, and the new one provides a relatively fresh start. Oftentimes, when transitioning from one lifetime to another, an individual may develop habits of thought that can aid him or her in the new setting. However, this can also be a deterrent in creating some of the new awareness required for new outcomes. All of this is achieved through painstaking re-workings of elements of a larger story that must be balanced in order to add to the greater harmony of All-That-Is. It is exactly for this reason that so many of you have had so many different lifetimes, and it is not unfair to recommend that you reconsider your options carefully before eliminating your choice of returning to this Earth plane, for it is indeed a treasure trove of opportunity. And it is opportunity each one of you strives for.

I am well aware of the pains and sorrows involved in childbirth and child rearing, attempts to live out one's dreams and illusions, and so on. It is all grist for the mill when applied to mastery of particular types of outcomes. For instance, let us say I drive a car very well, and yet I neglect to fasten my seat belt. I might receive a ticket for this, or a bruise, or a loss of physical ability, or even an ending of this lifetime, or simply a niggling insecurity about the possible outcome of this particular choice. Over time, I might become immune to concern over this action's negative potential, unless something else external happens to remind me, (a public awareness campaign, a neighbor's poor outcome . . .), or I suffer the negative impact myself. Still and all, I have chosen to live out this particular type of choice until I recognize and commit to a required change. If I never noticed negative possibilities, I would never consider increasing my skills in a particular manner. I also would not bother unless the skill impacted something of value to me, nor would I be inclined to value the skill unless I was rewarded in the doing of it, whether through pleasure, satisfaction in doing it, and/or the achievement of necessary gains from my point of view.

If all we ever do is think about our sorrows and difficulties, we cannot grow ourselves fully, nor have impetus to do so. We grow to express our Light, not to hide from darkness. Yet the contrast supplies a powerful fuel to keep us going, a rocket boost at times, and it is all perfect in the larger weave of All-That-Is. Because we have freedom of choice, our will requires our awareness of a full spectrum of options. Although many choices are ones to which we are predisposed, as well as chosen before entering our current life swell, it is helpful to remember that we are each being carried along a wave of opportunity, a wave we do our best to catch and form. However, if we don't quite make it, another will come along just behind it, perhaps even better suited to our true desires. If ever you feel caught up in confusion or chaos between one life swell or another, simply release your breath, sense your ability to float, and allow Life to serve you from below your awareness. For in truth, the larger part of you is still guiding and assisting you to attain greater mastery. And you will benefit eventually, whether you resist the new way or wave of opportunity, or go along with the flow. So ask yourself, "What do I truly consider meaningful in my life?" And hold your focus upon its essence more than the particulars that have come to light. You will find more peace in this, and greater capability for taking on new and more varied opportunities to ride this wave to fruition, to increase your abilities in pre-chosen areas, and to unfold a fuller expression of who you really are and what you came to be/do in this lifetime.

I trust you will complete your mission exactly as designed to fulfill your greater role in the Cosmos. For that is all there is—experiencing, unfolding, riding waves of frequency. Though names and particulars may change, experiencing is Eternal. As are each one of you.

And so I shall retire from this conversation for now. Take note of all that follows it for you personally, for your personal line of thinking on this subject matter can serve you well.

I remain, as always, Mo-Ray of the Archangelic Kingdom, Speaker of Truth, Show-er of the Way and Facilitator of True Beingness in this World of Opportunity. I thank you for your assistance and agreements around this, and I am loving you, and helping you, all-ways!!!!!

9/17/13

Good morning, Dear One! I am Mo-Ray of the Archangelic Kingdom, Speaker of Truth, Show-er of the Way and Analyzer of Peace-Creating Attributes. I have come today to assist you in rectifying your own heart and mind. In the past, you have many times judged your own actions, as well as that of others, as "good" or "evil." Whether you actually utilized these terms in your mind is immaterial. The outcome remains the same. And as I have discussed with you, certainly it is important to recognize the relative amounts of light expressed by a thought, action or situation, and indeed it can be a very valuable catalyst for your growth and development. However, once the growth has been triggered, it is time to assist yourself by loosening the hold that judgment has upon you.

For instance, if I had hit my thumb with a hammer accidentally, I would have a powerful catalyst for taking more caution in the future. In fact, it's imperative for my self-growth, otherwise my trust for myself becomes impaired. But once I have recognized the need for caution, no further catalyst is required, and it would behoove me to accept the experience as a catalyst for growth rather than to continue berating myself for the original lack of caution, i.e. "beating myself up." (As if the first method of self-injury had not been enough!) This is more than unnecessary, it is a negative occurrence, in which many of you indulge regularly, and it is time to let this pattern go, so you may live in Truth, not neglect or self-abandonment. Heaven on Earth does not have a place for such activities.

When I tell you something is lacking in light, it does not mean it is awful. It means it is a catalyst for expressing more Light, for recognizing that more Light is required in order to create and maintain Heaven on Earth. Once you have recognized this, you can truthfully affirm "I have learnt such-and-such," or "I am practicing or developing my skills at such-and-such."

Similarly, when you recognize a need for the expression of greater light in the actions of another, or in a situation, simply affirm what the being is ultimately seeking to develop, if this seems clear to you; acknowledge respectfully to yourself that the person is engaged in a learning process, as we all are; and consider what you might be asking yourself to learn in response to his or her action, particularly if you find yourself responding through negative emotions. Also, when a situation appears to be expressing a low level of light, consider what kind of a catalyst it may be for those involved, and what positives it might be a catalyst for

for you to grow in yourself. This will help to accelerate the process, and dissuade you from "task-tasking" over the affair, as so often occurs, and which only further decreases the amount of Light expression involved. You don't make yourself "right" or "good" by proving the "wrong" or "evil" of another being's actions, or of a turn of events in your world. If this course of action seems improbable to you, simply consider this, "Will I do better by complaining about something or by developing my own ability to shine my own Light more clearly and take appropriate action based upon this Light's requirements?" Then let all flow as it will.

If you desire assistance releasing judgment, first recognize it as part and parcel of your own search for Truth, rather than "negativizing" it further, and invite your angels to help here. They can assist you greatly, in the timing and manner most appropriate for you. In the meantime, simply ease up on the topic as best you can, and recognize yourself as a pure expression of Divine Light in development, and trust your own growth process.

I would also like to tell you that the day will come when it is very easy to let such judgments go. Think of this as "Non-Judgment Day," if you like, and know that there are many powerful forces, including your own Higher Will, working in concert to prepare the way for this time, which some have referred to as the Peace of a Million Years of Dreaming. I want you to know you have been selected, and have chosen, a most particular role in this that well suits you. You can choose any number of ways to carry it through, but the role's essence is quite finely honed by eons of developing true self-expression. And it is good.

I love you with all my heart and I am a part of who you really are. My thanks to you, all-ways, for scribing at this time, and for trusting in our process together.

I remain as always, Mo-Ray of the Archangelic Kingdom, Speaker of Truth, Show-er of the Way, and I am designed to recognize the many aspects of Light in All Creation.

And I am loving and calling upon the Light in each one of you to self-create the world of Your Own Highest Good and that of All-That-Is.

And so it is. Blessed be.

9/19/13

Good morning, Dear One! I am Mo-Ray of the Archangelic Kingdom, Speaker of Truth, Show-er of the Way, Mother of the Lady Mary Magdalene and Keeper of Harmony through Awareness. I have come today to tell you I am very aware of the happenings upon the Earth plane today and I am doing everything I can to assist in harmonizing the varied vibrations responding to one another chaotically, in order to allow resolution to naturally arise. I do not meddle in particular expressions of discord. I work completely on the etheric level to assist, along with many others, including those of higher overall vibration than my own. I have come to you once or twice before specifically to help you to raise your own vibration—one time that you recall most particularly, when in a school parking lot upon your first visit to the Upper Peninsula,[7] and the other during a particularly helpful energetic healing session from your friend Auriel.[8] There were others involved as well; however I was the "lead player," as it were.

I share this with you so you might understand more specifically, more tangibly, what I am referring to when I say "harmonizing frequencies." I do not change anyone's mind or emotions. I work solely at the frequency level and usually the being entrains very well with this, and many positive outcomes occur on all levels, some more obviously and others more subtly. You have been trained in this as well, and are quite adept beyond your conscious knowing of this. You assist by exemplifying and exuding a gentle harmony, a flow of Grace, regardless of any inequities within your system, because it is your fundamental nature. You chose this at a cellular level when you arose from the Great Womb of All-That-Is. And you have trained yourself to radiate this aspect of who you are more strongly with each successive lifetime in ALL WORLDS. Because of this, harmonizing frequencies is your natural state, and it has been magnified by the choices you have made over eons of existence.

---

[7] *This was at a point when it seemed I would be unable to move to Michigan's Upper Peninsula and be with the man with whom I'd fallen deeply in love. I was extremely miserable. I picked up the book I was reading, Alan Cohen's* The Dragon Doesn't Live Here Any More, *and upon reading the title of the next chapter,* The Power of Positive Thinking, *I thought "I just cannot do this!" and closed the book. Seconds later, I suddenly felt happy, though there had been no discernible change of any kind in my situation, and no effort on my part to move out of my despair. Shortly afterward, I listened to a phone message that turned the external situation around, eventually bringing me my heart's desire.*

[8] *This healing session with Auriel Coleman in the late '90s brought through a powerful activation of energy for my life's mission, and was another turning point in my life.*

This does not mean you are without issues, or that you have never wronged another, or been frightened, panicked or enraged. It simply means that this is your natural baseline, and this baseline has continued to raise itself due to your choice.

Any angst you feel regarding what I have shared so far is solely due to vows you have taken in the past to remain private, in order to work more fully behind the scenes. It is TIME TO REMOVE THE VEIL AND BE TRULY SEEN!!!!! The "VIEW" does help others, as well as your own self, because this privacy has become the womb from which it is time to birth now. You will always be safe, and you will always be protected, for your time in the dungeons of existence are over. Indeed, it is far more "safe" and protective for you to allow those energies that suit you to flow fully outward, and vice versa. The timing is a natural one. It is understood that you are in a natural process that is three-quarters of the way through the birth canal. If you choose to accelerate this process, know that you cannot go wrong. Simply trust that this is Truth for you, and allow yourself to take your next step forward.

I put down my pen and felt myself move through a sense of old energetic nets, as my energy field expanded bit by bit, leading to a wonderful feeling of freedom, a sense of stretching outward and being solidly present and visible in a new way.

We applaud you for the energetic shift you have just made. Enjoy!!!! There is more yet to come—this is *only* the beginning!!!!

I leave you with this for now: Walk with your head held high, knowing you have come solely for the good of All-That-Is, including your more personal self, and that you are creating a NEW VERSION of REALITY with each step you take, a step into experiencing more and more of Heaven on Earth. This is how it comes to fruition – each new step forward, each circle 'round the bend into Higher Awareness, Greater Truth, Increased Stability and STRONG AND FULLER NATURALLY-ARISING EXPRESSIONS OF LOVE, JOY, BEAUTY, FREEDOM!!!!!!!

I thank you for taking these notes, and sharing in energy together today. This day marks an important milestone for you. Mark it down and celebrate it always!

I remain, as always, Mo-Ray of the Archangelic Kingdom, as are you, Speaker of Truth, Show-er of the Way, Mother to the Lady Mary Magdalene, and Increaser of the Harmony of Vibration Within and Between *ALL,* and am here with you and part of you, loving you forever and all-ways!

9/20/13

Good morning, Dear One! I am Mo-Ray of the Archangelic Kingdom, Speaker of Truth, Show-er of the Way, Mother to the Lady Mary Magdalene and Keeper of the Flame of Wisdom within All Creation! I have come today to share with you the purpose of my stories—it is to activate the Divine Intelligence within all who read this, so they may more clearly and forthrightly receive their Highest Truths, and embody expression of them. The whole point of Mary Magdalene and Jesus the Christ's story was to awaken the world to the idea of Union and to their opportunity to move toward it most fully. It was an experiment that trained the vibrations of many to a higher realm of opportunity to embody their Highest Expression through opportunities for Union with the One-Is-All-Is-One. Unification will not obliterate individual experience or expression. It will embody them as part of itself with greater cohesion than ever before, because of the expansion of experience and the connection that foundations all.

It is this experience I seek to share with you today, that there is NO SEPARATION, simply expressions of the One carrying themselves into greater and greater experiences of wholeness, like tributaries pouring into vaster and vaster oceans of Beingness. Many times, the tributaries are directed in what seems to be a meandering fashion in the moment, trusting here and turning there, 'til they reach the ocean in view and realize each curve as part of the greater whole. Oftentimes, when one is called to turn away from another, or from an activity that appears to suit him or her, it is for a greater good to take hold down the road, because ultimately this one is turning toward something rather than away, although this something is not yet known to him or her consciously. There can be great turmoil in this one's response to this change, yet the turmoil itself is capable of being employed for the greater good, once one has aligned with the Truth of his being, accepted his feelings as such, and chosen to be a vehicle for the Higher Truth residing within him. Though its specific outcome be unknown, yet its essence remains clear—Union and the willingness to experience it, even when it appears to be farther away than home, yet it is home, in that Home ultimately is at its core. And you have so many opportunities before you to live out the fullness of who you are, in accordance with the Grand Design.

Your Union is at the core of your Divine Nature and it cannot be undone. When you assimilate newly activated aspects of who you really are, it can dislodge old wounds from their hidden places and call for resonance at a Higher Level. You then have the option of either ignoring such as best you can, which eventually allows a larger aspect of this theme or trauma to come to a head, or do your part to resolve it, though you may initially feel quite unhappy about dealing with it at all.

There are many tools available to each one of you for aiding you in this process. Most importantly, always know you are being assisted by those of us on your spiritual crew, and you can call upon us in any situation, no matter how hurtful or impossible it may appear to you. And know, please, that in time all will be in resolution and harmony will reign more fully than it yet has before.

So I may carry out your desires more purely, I ask that you call upon me with greater intensity and willingness to respond to my replies. And this is true for all of you and for all who desire to assist you from the Unseen Realms. Whenever you utilize our services, know that we are also fully and completely part of your selves, and that we hold your individual, unique essence in the very highest regard. I am communicating something vitally important for this time and place – assist yourself by knowing each one of you is loved without reservation, and cherished far beyond your conscious awareness of such.

That is all for now. I remain, as always, Mo-Ray of the Archangelic Kingdom, Speaker of Truth, Show-er of the Way, Mother to the Lady Mary Magdalene, and Keeper of the Flame of Wisdom Within All Creation, and I am loving you fully and completely, now and forever, all-ways!!!!

9/21/13

Good morning, and a very wonderful Autumnal Equinox to you, Dear One! I am, as you are now aware, "the Third Mary." I have been mainly hidden from public awareness 'til now to purpose. I am diligent in striving for the vision of Union for which my daughter, the Lady Mary Magdalene and her husband, Jesus the Christ, devoted their lives and essences. I have found my way to be in keeping with the Essene enclaves of yore, in which you utilized everything at your disposal with the least possible public presence, in order to avoid the resistance that may come from certain personality types to one's own, and to downplay any attempts to "pedestalize" the doer, i.e. put them above oneself, glorifying all their activities, which ultimately is a function of such ones' egos, seeking to borrow glory through association with the glorified one and to increase their own reputations by how well they aggrandize this one, rather than seeking and recognizing the Kingdom Within and the Divine birthright of All. Now, in this time of great awakening, the soul seeds of many are opening up and there is less "cult of the Divine," and increasing knowledge of the Kingdom Within. You are well-placed to receive my knowing, insights and points of view because you embody this aspect of neutrality, understanding yourself as neither "greater than" or "less than" so well, and because it is time for you to come more fully into public awareness from this ego-free space, so you may bring my Truths forward with fullness, along with many of the other gifts and potentials you carry. I ask for your patience with the continued gradual unfoldment of my tale. It is laced with many opportunities for greater awakening, and as this is our purpose, there is no point in rushing to its conclusion and stripping much of such away, is there?

You are knowing me from the inside out because you embody many of my traits and desires. You witness the path of others well, you feel your knowing within you, you ask for clarification when necessary, you know your limits as well as your passions, you understand you are always growing in wealth of love, you ameliorate change, transitions, with Grace, you exacerbate the knowing within all others, you exude much charge for allowing natural processes to unfold, you wait, albeit not always patiently, for Divine Timing. You tune in to what is best for the greater whole, in most cases. You allow yourself time to assimilate change and for "course corrections" to become clear to you before attempting to navigate them. You trust your instincts and you utilize them well. You can tell what feels "on track" and "off." You know your inner guidance system well. You know your love is important fuel, a catalyst for growth. You understand the inner workings of the human mind. You allow all things to be of their nature, as opposed to trying to pull them into aspects they are not. You're efficient in your use of Divine Timing. And you're well aware of the ill effects of pushing the river.

I am opening a doorway to you now to understand better my current world. I ask you to use your intelligence in coming through gradually, and not rattling your personal energy system too much.

I stopped writing and closed my eyes. I felt the energy shift and a sense of a wide, rounded, earthen doorway within my mind's eye. I had the sense of putting my hands out and feeling its thick, manmade side. I sensed a night sky sort of feel, but fuller, with a sense of a great variety of energies in it to the area past this threshold. I felt myself put my right foot through this doorway, then back again. I was testing it out, and asked how I would maintain my ability to return fully to my current time/space reality. I became aware of the silver cord running from the base of my spine all the way deep into the core of the Earth. I had a sense of sort of pole vaulting from it, leaping upward as it extended with me, into the consciousness of the one who'd been speaking with me. It was all light there, a soft full light encompassing me that spread throughout my upper chest and lightened the rest of me with it. I basked in this for a few moments, then became aware of multiple energy pathways, tube-like paths with substance to them, connecting this consciousness to different aspects of the world. I chose one that connected to our household, and experienced an energetic view of our home and its occupants. I returned to the central consciousness, then chose another pathway to view the household of a close friend whom I was told would welcome this visit, briefly experiencing her energy and that of her home. I knew this was enough for now, and returned to the central consciousness of Mo-Ray, shifting from there back to regular awareness of my own time space reality.

Now that you have experienced my world more fully, and clarified and strengthened your conscious connection with it, do you better understand our purpose of Union?

Yes.

That is good! Now go forth and enjoy your day with abandon! We shall expand on our connection more, and our Truth, in the near future. Namaste!

I remain, as always, Mo-Ray, Mirandella, "the Third Mary," Speaker of Truth, Show-er of the Way and Lover of the Instinct of Union within All Creation!

9/22/13

Good morning, Dear One! I am Mary, Mother of the Lady Mary Magdalene, Speaker of Truth, Show-er of the Way and Relater of Tales that Tell the Activities of Light Taking Form on your planet. I have come today to take you into my keeping in order to relate better to the time of the Lady Mary Magdalene's birth and upbringing.

Things were simpler then, in the sense that there were not nearly as many choices to make regarding daily affairs, but much tougher because we were not allowed to make certain of those choices available to us without severe consequences, both materially and socially. Once a transgression from the norm had occurred, there was no going back, no fresh start for the so-called wrongdoer. And it was the same for all of us, even those born within the Goddess tradition. There were practices we were taught to subscribe to without questioning, and others not allowable, though it was clear to me there were a few privately exploring such options. This in itself could not be brought out into the open, discussed through conversation, without dire consequences as well. The freedom of exploration you all desire was very confined during this time on Earth and none of us shared ourselves completely openly without fear of backlash against some viewpoint that did not fit with that of our unit, be it coven, family or tribe. All except the Lady Mary Magdalene. And in myself, there was an iron-strong ability to stand up to such, but only to purpose, and my purpose was to raise the Lady Mary up in such a way that she might have a strong foundation from which to carry forth hers. She was largely free of the fear of such consequences, though she was aware she would experience some of them at the appropriate point. She obeyed the law of her source and of her own Divine Nature, and I accepted this as a matter of course. And it was understood in our family unit that I was always watching out for her, guarding and supporting her freedom in whatever ways possible to me. And I knew, I was even able to see and feel at times, the immense protection that surrounded her, like a great buzz of angels, ancient guardians and certain elemental energies.

Lady Mary was not inhibited in sharing her love of all creation and her joy of being, and this was disarming to many who would have otherwise seen her as "wrong" and responded in ways common for such. As she grew, so did her charm and beauty, as well as her questioning of common ways and law.

She asked me once why I did not do the same, for she knew me well enough to understand that we saw things very similarly. It was a testing sort of question, for she was well aware of the nature of our destiny together and of the ways of our society. I explained that I forswore my personal viewpoints to be beyond rebuke so that when the time came of resistance to her activities, I could rally forces on her behalf to dissuade those who would seek to hold her back and limit her experience, so that she might better unfold her purpose. The pristine reputation of our family would delay any retribution typically required by certain of her actions, and give her time to surround herself with allies. Young Mary was fifteen at the time of her asking, and quite bold for anyone her age, whether male or female. And I trusted her implicitly, for I knew her core and her willingness, nay passion, to be of great service to the whole. She was bound to this and her apparent freedom served it well. In the interim, she enjoyed life with all of us—her three brothers, (two older and one younger), and two younger sisters—Martha and Miriam. There was a fourth boy, but he died in childbirth and that was the last of them to be birthed through me.

Martha was terribly unhappy as a young child—petulant and always feeling left out, left behind the others. I'd hoped that once she had a younger sister to play with that this would disappear. But she never truly related to Miriam, only as a little doll. Other than that, she experienced Miriam as more of a bother to her, and another for others to prefer paying attention to, rather than herself. And it was true that Martha was not well-liked because of her petulant ways and acts of vindication.

Please do not misunderstand. I loved her dearly, as I did all my children. However, I was aware that despite my efforts, and the times when she was truly at peace in her world, feeling loved and accepted, that hers was not a charitable nature, and that she would be quite challenged to grow into the fullness of the love within her. I am amazed that her story is not told more often, for it describes a part of each of you, though perhaps a part that you prefer to hide away, in that she carried envy to a visible extreme and paid the price of that. Hers was not an evil nature. She simply was not aware of how beloved and lovable she truly was, and paid more attention to comparing the kinds of benefits that attracted others to them, than to discovering her own worthy nature.

And so it goes. Your world has been rife with those so bent on exploring what others have that they've neglected their own nature and its true development. Each of you holds special keys, certain gifts, that can help unlock the plenty available, the many treasures awaiting you, through establishing Heaven on Earth. And each of you holds in trust the core of your own essence, which it is TIME TO BRING FORTH FULLY NOW AND LIVE IN THE EXPANDED CONSCIOUSNESS OF THE ONE-IS-ALL-IS-ONE!!!!! This is your real "tribe," if ever there was one. This is where your allegiance belongs and where your liberation is key to the song of its heart. I know each of you is growing in accord with your own soul nature and that you are not capable of holding it back much longer. Sing your song NOW, and be proud of your holy birthright in Divinity, as part of the true tribal creation, the real know-how of Being. This is your time to shine your Light fully and freely. Allow no doubts or lingering beliefs in unworthiness to hold you back. Your harmony is the star of creation and your own willingness to believe in your ability to BE WHO YOU ARE and shine your Light freely and fully is KEY!

Martha was not ready to do so then. Are you willing to do so now? It is imperative for your own freedom and that of humankind. And it is forthcoming because that is the way of things. The evolution is here, now, and every slant of the sun reminds your self of this and assists you in carrying it out. We all on the "Other Side" are here working with you, for your freedom is our own as well. We have invested ourselves in assisting with this shift, this rearrangement through time and space, as part of our own individual destinies and purpose. We are all amazed by the stunning array of Light being brought forth as we assist you, and you assist yourselves, in this Liberation time. And I thank you for your scribing so diligently and accurately, as I lay down my tales to share with you.

I love you forever and onward and in all-ways. I remain in Truth, Love and Justice, the Third Mary, Mother of the Lady Mary Magdalene, Mo-Ray of the Archangelic Kingdom, Speaker of Truth, Show-er of the Way and Keeper of the Flame that Activates the Light Within All Humanity and Beyond. And I am with you, and part of you, all-ways!!!!

9/22/13, 6:15 pm

Hello again, Dear One! Yes, I understand you want to record the highlights of our inner conversation from later in the day. You heard me refer to Martha's vindictive nature and its dire consequences. It was she who told the people where Mary Magdalene was when they went to stone her. She was not told of their plan, but she knew they were not happy with Mary. And she knew no one else close to Mary would have willingly shared her whereabouts at this tense time, for reasons supposedly unknown.

No one in the family trusted her again. Martha was shunned, especially by her own father, once he heard of this group's intended mistreatment of Mary. He had always had great misgivings about Mary's forthrightness and questioning of the status quo, but he loved her deeply and feared for her welfare. He was a tough man, determined to "stick to his guns," as you say, which made him all the more loyal. And he was a faithful provider, a staunch supporter of all he believed was right, a good man. He and I were not the most loving of partners, but that was not the main goal for many couples then. We were loyal to one another and would not have parted ways, had it not been for my desire to follow through with my goal of helping Mary the Younger. And so came the rift between us, not due to my desire to assist Mary, which he understood well, but for his being left without me, he who had done no wrong to me and felt sheltered by my care. We understood one another, supported the welfare of one another, and worked as a team in those ways available to us in our society, without great fanfare or emotion. We trusted one another's stalwart ways. So for me to later abandon him, in his eyes, to help someone else, though it be our daughter, to put him second, nee third, was no trifling matter.

I could not do otherwise. When the time came, I had to know Mary was safely out of the country, though I knew I would not see her again in this lifetime. Her welfare, her upbringing, her ability to work in tandem with Jesus the Christ, my help in facilitating this, was the central purpose of my life, the core of my world's creation. I can understand Martha's resistance, knowing deep down that no one in our family cared for her in quite the way I cared for Young Mary. And I could not help it, though I loved Martha and all of my brethren dearly as my own. Still, I am aware of my role in Martha's choosing the role she did. And I knew Mary the Younger would be cast out eventually. It was written in the stars, as were many other deeds.

And so it was. I knew I could not do other than what I did and be in integrity with my chosen purpose, yet I knew great sorrow for its impact on others. My heart was meant for Mary first, and all else second. And this is how it was. Fortunately, I was also aware of the Great Life Stream that carries us all, and that eventually we would all come together in Union as part of the Grand Design. We have explored many options through and beyond the "Other Side" for examining cause and effect, the influence that one's actions may have upon others, and the key here is whether or not the core intention be love. And if it is not, all of Heaven and Earth cannot be bound to it. If it is, and ultimately, most often it is, eventually what appears broken will come back together again.

Now, this being the case, I laid my worries aside as well as I was able, and followed my heart's guiding to where Mary waited by the sea with her companions to take her over to what you now call Europe. She knew Union would be supported there eventually, and in the meantime, the nature of this new location would support her and her growing family. For she was pregnant, and this passage could not fail her. I was allowed to hug her good-bye, give her my last tokens of ancient Goddess practices for safekeeping, and share my essence with her in person for the final time while we were in these human forms. I trusted my love to serve her well, near or far, and knew she could better address her life's later purpose removed from our current political hell. It was for her to seed the frequency of Union wherever and whenever possible, so it might blossom forth and multiply when the "gardeners" arrived to care for it. She was, and is, a very courageous soul. And I am grateful to have known and stuck by her.

That is enough for now. I wish you well, my Dear One. Please go and enjoy your husband, and know it will not be long 'til we take up our story again.

I remain, as ever, the Third Mary of the Feminine Trinity, Mo-Ray of the Archangelic Kingdom, Mirandella of your own heart, Speaker of Truth, Show-er of the Way, Mother to the Lady Mary Magdalene and Enlightener of All Who Choose the Way of Union. And I am loving each of you, forever and all-ways!!!

9/23/13

Good morning, Dear One! I am Mary the Elder, Mother of the Lady Mary Magdalene, Speaker of Truth, Show-er of the Way and Highlighter of all that assists Your Personal Evolution. I have come today to ascertain your field of abundance—what grows well for you and how you might assist yourself to share this ability with other areas of your life.

When you came into this world, you came equipped with an umbilicus connecting you with all the physical nourishment you required. After the birthing, your nourishment came by way of your mother's milk, or a facsimile thereof, and eventually this arena became broader, including specially prepared foods and eventually a complete range of them. With the increasing complexity of choices came less guarantee of appropriate nutrition, but also great possibility for it, along with great diversity of taste, texture, preference and so on.

It is the same in other areas of your life—greater choice, greater freedom, greater ease of motion, less guarantee of safety and/or fulfillment, greater possibilities for variety, adventure, fulfillment and achievement of goals.

When you embark upon a new experience, ask yourself, "Shall I promote my welfare and/or that of others in this manner? Do I enjoy the newness of this choice? Am I open for a fresh experience? Will I absorb the most helpful aspects of what this new experience has to offer? Can I fully let go into it to reap its benefits more plentifully? Am I capable of fresh awareness, with minimal filtering by my culturally limited thinking? Will I adjust to the qualities of this experience in such a way that I might be said to begin to embody them? Will I allow myself this ability to merge with that which I greatly value? Am I holding on to a more restricted version of who I am out of fear of newness? Can I relate to the transitioning, the adjustment possible, when I allow myself to expand into larger, more complex forms of creation, knowing I am still my core self, and that I am simply allowing this self to explore a more expansive playing field? Do I trust who I am enough to allow myself to explore fuller options of living? Am I willing to become a vaster version of myself, so that I may continue growing my ability to influence positive change? Where am I in this flow of potential right now? Am I going in the direction of expanded, Light-filled choices, or have I remained stuck in the mud of my own belief in negative causes and ill effects?"

I am championing you, your growth and capability, because I know your core, your essence, well enough to realize its ability to serve upon larger and larger playing fields, to hear it calling you forth to explore and experience vaster degrees of consciousness. Simply by considering such, you can experience your consciousness's growth. And I am aware of your utility in bringing Heaven on Earth more easily, in a fully grounded and accessible fashion, through your expanded empowerment in this arena.

You will have more and more choices to expand upon as you allow yourself a greater field of opportunity, an expanded diversity of abundance, a less limited version of daily reality, as you continue to utilize your human form and all the wonders of daily living in your current space/time reality. I am aware of the growth of each one of you in this area, of consciousness field exploration, and exhort you to continue more rapidly so you may bring more Grace and expanded opportunity to your experience of anchoring Heaven on Earth.

I witness you with great respect and appreciation, as you respond to the challenges inherent in transitioning your world. And I am grateful for your willingness to be a part of this great expansion, this movement into greater Union/Oneness with All-That-Is. I am here for you, at all times and in all-ways, loving you and cheering you forward, as you feed your passion for living truly and fully in this space/time playing field, absorb your Higher Good into all that you do, and elevate your love and compassion to the level of genius-hood. I am grateful to be here as part of your world. Live Life fully and no significant regret is possible.

I remain, as always, Mary the Elder, Mother of the Lady Mary Magdalene, Speaker of Truth, Show-er of the Way and Allower of All that is Unbound Beauty, and I am grateful for your world and your part in it. I love each one of you, forever and all-ways, and I will speak with you again in this manner soon.

9/24/13

Good morning, Dear One! I am Mo-Ray of the Archangelic Kingdom, Mary the Elder, Mother of the Lady Mary Magdalene, Speaker of Truth, Show-er of the Way and Specializer in Igniting the Passion for Union which exists within All Creation. I have come today to tell you more of my personal story. It behooves you to complement this with certain aspects of your own, as foretold.

In the very, very long ago, there abided one who loved dearly, so dearly that all this one desired was for all to live together in the spirit of cooperation, in Union, twenty-four hours a day, seven days a week, and then some. This desire was so strong that it pulled her at every opportunity to open more and more of her heart chakra. In the process, her heart chakra metamorphosed in such a way that it began to invite whole beings into it, with all of their ways and aspects, which were already quite diverse. This expansion eventually reached the point of busting, which it did, in such a way that future members of our human race were seeded with elements of this one's heart chakra. You and I are among those, and this is why we are especially passionate about the goal of living Heaven on Earth. It's what we came for. We are designed to carry it forward. Its essence, its seed kernel, was implanted in us long before our births into physicality. And this is becoming the norm, as the many who were originally seeded touched the lives of many more and shared their attributes with them. In many cases, this kernel lay dormant for a very long time. Now it is awakening and spreading throughout humanity and beyond. It is very important that we all remember we are the children of Source, all created by the same factor, which is LOVE, and as such, it is time to grow more fully into this likeness. We are the Chosen Ones, chosen to blossom into this Love Nature as never before. We are all gifted with a unique vibration, a unique quality or aspect of our Love Source, and so it is vitally important that we each move it forward, branch it out there, radiate it more fully and frequently, to accelerate the advancing Divine Union, the coming into wholeness, that is slated for fruition.

I am very happy to let you know we are almost there. I feel and live in its about-to-spring forth nature, as when many rains have come in early spring and you know that once the sun breaks through those clouds, abundant blossoms will be a-popping. It is time, therefore, to look at aspects of the history we have accrued, to shine a light on them, so to speak, so we may receive the nuggets, reap the wheat, recognize the gold in and resulting from these experiences. When I suggest this, it is with great respect for our readers' individual stories, parts of which they may still wish to hide from their own view or ignore. Look from the framework of Forever into these key moments without judgment. Put the judgment aside and ask yourself, "What good has come from this? What strengths did I and others develop in response to this? What of my own values were revealed to me by my response to this transgression? How have I created good by honoring those values since? What do I strive to create today, based upon this experience? And how do the echoes of this creation process influence those around me?"

When you have discovered your answers to these questions, you will have discovered many profound truths for your life. I am sharing all this with you because I am quite familiar with such life reviews and the substance they carry for reworking past issues and consolidating positive changes already in progress. If I were to tell you every nuance of my heart's desires, they would calculate into more grains of sand than your thinking mind could grab hold of, yet they would all be representative of one thing—TO GROW HARMONY MORE FULLY WITHIN/WITHOUT, such that the experience of Divine Union, the Living of Heaven on Earth, is freely and fully chosen.

And so it is. You can delineate it further through your communications with me, but this encompasses the entirety of the story. And so I am complete with our form of sharing in this way for now.

I remain, as always, Mirandella of your heart, Mo-Ray of the Archangelic Kingdom, "The Third Mary," Mother of the Lady Mary Magdalene, Speak-er of Truth, Show-er of the Way and Delineator of Key Elements of the Road Home. And I am loving you, all of you, all-ways and forever.

9/25/13

Good morning, Dear One! I am Mo-Ray of the Archangelic Kingdom, Mirandella of Your Heart, "The Third Mary," Mother of the Lady Mary Magdalene, Speaker of Truth, Show-er of the Way and Initiator of All Beings' Revival into Oneness, as are each one of you when you "sacrifice" egoic concerns to re-member your wholeness and trust your relationship with the Source of All Good. When I come to you, you allow me to bring your heart into your experience of your elemental good. This is because of my own nature's alignment with Truth you have been seeking for a very long time. I uphold the aspects of your nature that allow one-hundred percent freedom of exploration of your essence and its wealth of potential good. I allow your exploration into the nature of cause and effect to be assisted by examining it more thoroughly and experiencing it through the lens beyond your time/space reality. I know you are accepting your experience when you are willing to retain its nuggets consciously for future growth. And I am requiring your equal opportunity to lift up your sight to include Heaven in your daily experiences, as part and parcel of your own Divine Nature, and the inherent vibrations therein.

I am giving you this information because very soon you will be changing from your "doing" orientation to that of "being." Your activities will become infused with your intentions much more noticeably. It will be unavoidably clear. And so it would behoove you to clean up any "messes," residues, etc. of old, unwanted habits or patterns, so you can create more fully, more pleasingly, to your soul's nature, through your Light's capacity for clarity, integrity and exceptional exhilaration.

When you create more fully through the Light that you are, all the world echoes with greater alignment with that part of you that you have burst forth into the three-dimensional realm. And you are better equipped, therefore, to create the next work from alignment, and the next, and the next, so that the exponential growth is tremendous! Your art has gifted the Universe such Grace, such dear embodiment of vast essence, that we know you will fulfill its potential, we know you will experience its impact upon humanity, and therefore, on all else in your world. We have appreciated all the efforts required for each step along the way, and know there is great Love coordinating all future endeavors entrusted to your care for its being suitably shared in your world. And we are appreciating all the growth, all the activated potential, required for such. It will behoove you to set down on paper all you envision for your art's experience in the world and to check back in with this from time to time. We are exposing you to this information to purpose, so you may chart your course with such most clearly and effortlessly, in the sense that you feel the current buoying up your movement in this direction. And it will behoove you to recognize the link between that related book and this one more clearly now. We trust you understand the Love of the Universe that invites both projects to come into form as part of who you are and who you are becoming.

So I would ask you, when do you experience the greatest unfoldment of your love nature? When you are engaged in activity that suits you, or when you are engaged in putting up with what you do not desire? Are you working to minimize one over the other? Are you requiring others to do the same to be in your good graces, or are you allowing, going with the flow, of the relationship, the interaction between others' Highest Good choices and your own? How much LOVE do you want to experience in this lifetime? And how much are you willing to own your choices through truth, freedom and response-ability? If you are doubting your own path at any time, remember—you are the restorer of your Garden through your exploration of this time/space realm and its antecedents as a matter of course. It cannot be otherwise, even during those times when it appears completely torn up. This is the "aeration" process that helps you till your soil for fertile growth, and when you are ready, those clear intentions that have already taken root will show themselves in the light, sprouting fruitfully. Your willingness to design your Garden energetically will allow you to come into wholeness most fully through interaction of your soul seed's germination, the love that you are part of and carry, and the intrinsic qualities you have chosen to re-member through your lifetime with the Divine Intention of your soul's calling, your part in the Grand Design, and your Higher Opportunities through trusting love and appreciation for the Higher Good of your counterparts, who are one with you.

Your willingness to be here, now, speaks greatly to your own definition of freedom, for it is ONLY through this self-allowing process that you can participate on the Earth plane. NEVER believe that you *have* to come back! It is an unparalleled opportunity that most of you have chosen over, and over, and over, and this is not out of foolishness, it is out of LOVE! Love for self and others, and gratefulness for this vast treasure-trove of possibility! Your existence now tells us you are willing to have a powerful impact upon human evolution because you are part of the great funneling into Union, you are part of the concordance, you are part of the "End Times" which allow for a new beginning!

When I tell you this, are you frightened or exhilarated? Do you trust you will land safely on the "other side" of this wholly enacted transition? Or are you concerned about tests of your fortitude, integrity, courage? If the latter is the case, remember that you have already passed through most of these gateways already and it is not "perfection" that is required, simply willingness to grow. All you encounter can help you raise yourself up through this process, if you choose to express the inner light of your being more rapidly. And you can enjoy this very much, because ultimately, it suits you! It is your harmony, your natural way of Being. And so it supports you most thoroughly. You are united with the expression of your own loving nature and this fulfills you! You are each unique in the strand of essence you carry, and your fulfillment is an indelible part of the Grand Design's wholeness. Continue your journey knowing you are beloved in all ways, and throughout all times and situations.

It is without reservation that I share this with you, for I am knowing the Love you are is supported by the many forms of Love you were sourced among, and it is good to contemplate this more frequently.

I am trusting your power to engage your Light with the momentum that is building for the great expansion now underway. And I am counting upon your Love's nature to reveal itself wholly and freely, upon its self-coordinated, well syncopated timing within the Symphony of Divine Exploration that is soon to crescendo throughout your world.

I am loving your experience of this new freedom within this world as it pertains to your dancing light display of being! Empower yourself now by knowing this experience is part of you and your future.

I am loving your touchstone of knowing your love is grounded in the elements of three-dimensional reality and integrating with the starshine that seeds its immortality. Your truth brings this experience closer to your now each moment. Your breath brings life to this freedom's foundation. Your knowing carries great love into great freedom of opportunity for expression throughout all realms, all states of Beingness, all willing harbingers of Harmony.

And so it is.

I remain, as always, Mo-Ray of the Archangelic Kingdom, "The Third Mary," Mother of the Lady Mary Magdalene, Speaker of Truth, Show-er of the Way, and Retainer of All That Nourishes Freedom's Keys. And I am loving you, all-ways and forever!

9/26/2013

Good morning, Dear One! I am Mo-Ray of the Archangelic Kingdom, "The Third Mary," Mother of the Lady Mary Magdalene, Mirandella of Your Heart, Speaker of Truth, Show-er of the Way and Keeper of the Flame Within the Hearts of All Humanity. I have come today to prepare you for your next physical journey, to meet your grandson Noah in person. I have selected you to be my emissary because you have shown yourself to be reliable through many lifetimes of service in one regard or another, and you are willing to lead others into more holistic understandings of Truth. You have proved yourself capable in many realms and on many levels, and this is why you have trusted yourself more than many yet do themselves in this lifetime.

It would appear you have not changed a baby before, but yet you have. It would appear you have not nursed, have not bathed, have not soothed a child before, but yet you have. You would not be expected to know the ins and outs, the ups and downs of being a new mother, and yet you do. It would behoove you to accept all this completely and live fully in the moment of this wonderful meeting in the flesh. It is a special moment that will not come again. When you look into his eyes, you will know all you would ever need to know about his soul's creation and your Union, your connection with one another.

If at any time you feel unsure about a situation with him, call upon my sense of awareness, look into your heart space, and recognize what your Inner Truth Sensor is showing you.

It will behoove you to know that all the realms are taking note of this great one's birth, and that you are being reminded daily of this truth; "Be only love, for that is what you are." Every time you call a name, any name, remember to bring this Truth into it, so you'll know everyone by his or her true appellation. And I can tell you it will magnify their acceptance of you and your appreciation of them greatly.

The next time you are experiencing hardship through your interaction with another, call upon your remembrance of this fact, breathe it into all your cells, and say your name as well as his or her own three times each, alternating them back and forth, with this awareness in mind. This will help you cohere the resonance, bring yourself into alignment with the Oneness factor, your Union within Source and throughout and beyond all timelines and dimensional fields of possibility. When you come into alignment with any particular aspect of Creation, you bring greater wholeness into your relationship with all aspects of Creation itself. And this is helping to bring the goal of Heaven on Earth here more rapidly.

I invite you to use this tool the next time you are out of sorts with any one of humankind and remember always to include yourself in the mix.

I am grateful we have had this time together this morning and, short as it may seem, it would behoove you to move on now with more vital aspects of your day.

I remain, as always, Mo-Ray of the Archangelic Kingdom, Mary the Elder, Mother of the Lady Mary Magdalene, Mirandella of your Heart, Speaker of Truth, Show-er of the Way, and Uniter of All Souls within the Perception of the Peace that surpasseth all understanding. And I am loving you, forever and all-ways.

THE THIRD MARY

9/27/13

Good morning to you, Dear Heart! I am Mo-Ray of the Archangelic Kingdom, "The Third Mary," Mother of the Lady Mary Magdalene, Speaker of Truth, Show-er of the Way and Delineator of Aspects of the New Meld of Mind and Heart coming into humanity's future. I am here today to share with you a little bit about the "Mary" factor. I have titled myself "The Third Mary," not chronologically, as you know, but in regards to public awareness. I am still the progenitor of the Lady Mary Magdalene, who precedes me in being sought for assistance and inspiration, and who is better known due to her relatively controversial nature, relative to how *others* see her, that is. I am quite sure she finds herself sought after by some more for notoriety's sake than for purely spiritual interest; however, I will not dwell upon that today. She is a shining light whose willingness to be clear, available, and serve throughout the Universe is unmatched by any before her. And she is participating *now* in her assistance with human evolution at this time in many powerful ways.

Ask yourself, the next time you recognize your ability to stand strong in who you are, regardless of what any others might think, not with strands of martyrdom, "better than" or outrage, "Who set the stage for this in the world? Who set the precedent so clearly that I know I am not alone in this aspect of Creation? Who set an example so strong I can draw upon it at any time?" It was the pair of them—the Lady Mary Magdalene and Jesus the Christ. Though clearly Jesus's story has been altered to emphasize his suffering and therefore, his martyrdom, this came only after the fact. His immortal soul chose his path and his human willingness carried it through, despite the hardships he encountered. It was the same for my daughter, the Lady Mary Magdalene. She knew Jesus the Christ from the time he was quite young. They played together and betrothed privately, i.e. shared their thoughts of love and commitment at an early age—nine (Mary) and six (Jesus).

They didn't know I was looking in on them, checking on how everything was going. They knew they would have many moons to unravel their story together, and many more to glory in their vast love and appreciation for Creation in and around our world. Yet they also felt vitally drawn to be together as much as it was possible in those early days. Their play was thoroughly imbued with the Love of Spirit and the aspects of nature that spoke willingly to them and through them. The interplanetary harmonic streams between them were greatly activated by their time outdoors together, and fueled and solidified their purpose. The Lady Mary Magdalene was bound to explore her experience of other realms through her play time with him, so it was quite extraordinary to witness. Whenever they were together, the Light shining between them grew and grew, stronger with each meeting, such that those with eyes to see were more than dazzled, and everyone gave them a wide berth from which they were able to have more privacy than would be typical. It behooved them to spend this time together well, for the troubles of childhood were small, and their knowing of their bond together huge, so they were able to breathe in the Spirit of this with ease.

As the Light between them increased, so did the planetary elation with them and their learning of sacred ways to interact with and reap many benefits from the natural world grew exponentially. But most of all, they experienced the joy of their fairly unfettered time together.

Martha was quite put out by this, of course. She did not want to have less of her sister's attention, never mind the Young Adonis/cherub adored, so clearly smitten with her sister. Martha did not try to come between them, for that was not conceivable, even for her, at this time. But she pouted grandly and bore ill will to their partnership, while at the same time honoring its ability to help bring us all home to Heaven on Earth. For she wanted this badly, more than I think even she was aware of, yet she did not truly grasp the ways one must undergo to create it, the letting go of the personal desire into the transpersonal will, which can create the sort of harmony the personal self truly desires. Martha exemplified contradiction. She was a contradiction even to herself, yet she was so caught up in what she thought others had which she did not, and what she thought they thought of her, that she did not come to clarity, to peace within herself, for a very long time. And she knew her abilities would bring her all she sought if she trusted them, but she was overwhelmed with grief over not being able to command the attention that some others knew, and this drew her away from their development. She could only be at peace when she knew her time was done on this Earth, for the time being, and that she would carry on beyond it, eventually to make right what she had not become capable of during this human lifetime.

It was a noble desire that brought Martha here, to ground her nature in the physical realm, learn through her challenges to experience more growth of self-love and self-acceptance, such that it might empower others to shine as well. It was a tough road for her on the Earth plane.

She was quite troubled by her own lack of commitment to the Light over the pressures created by her conscious thinking mind and wounded heart, wounded by envy and self-doubt. She illustrated many character flaws that so many have grappled with and continue to since. Yet hers was a loving nature, simply overwhelmed at times by her negative inclinations.

I am truly regretful that I was not able to guide her better through her challenges, yet I knew I must invest my energies elsewhere—to the household in general, and the upbringing of the Lady Mary Magdalene within the Goddess tradition and beyond, the best I was able. I would not go against this soul choice, and she, Martha, ultimately understood that this was so. We each had the burden and the gifts, the response-ability of the choices we made in the Swing Between the Worlds. And we are all in Union together, connected within the One-Is-All-Is-One, in which no competition or injustice is available.

Soon you will witness this factor becoming more tangibly prevalent in your world. For now, suffice it to say you are all becoming more well integrated units of Spirit into form. And I am delighted to be a part of your experience and a witness of it.

I want to speak with you of the "Third Mary-hood," and I shall. It was pre-ordained that we work in Trinity together—Maiden, Mother, Crone. Though we, of course, all had our time in each, still, the youngest of our three, the Lady Mary Magdalene, enriched the embodiment of Maiden in a new way, glorifying the aspects of freedom to do and be; the "Mother Mary" as she is known, adding to the Goddesshood of progenitorship, and myself bringing more energetic impact to the legacy of Crone, the great educator and wisdom being. Believe me, we *all* have taken all of these roles and may merge them at will. It is in the harmony and interaction between all three that a Trinity is interwoven. We are a Trinity because we enact fuels of growth within and between our Divine Natures, and it behooves us to express our divinity in such a way that you will allow yourself to take part in it, to be One with it, to be purely affected by it, so your own Light Nature may bubble out more easily and grandly.

I am saying these things so you may better appreciate your own God/Goddesshood, because you are all part of the Light of the One-Is-All-Is-One. We merely share symbolic roles together so we might more purely express our individual strands in tandem with the greater hologram of Life upon this planet and beyond.

We are knowing that you are part of "we," as well as of other units and aspects of your unique Divine Nature, and this is all that is here for you in this now, every moment. For it is foretold that all worlds shall be "unionized," shall come together as one, and so we impart to you this knowing, so it may resound with the Truth in the Core of you, reverberate grandly, and help further activate your knowing and growing of Heaven on Earth by fueling your part in the Grand Design.

And so it is. That is enough for today. We look forward to speaking with you again on the morrow.

We are the Trinity of Love, Light and Wisdom on the Earth Plane, carried forth in Human, Feminine form symbolically to assist in the Great Merging, and I am showing you the way of glory by my example and its reflection of your own.

I am Mo-Ray of the Archangelic Kingdom, Mirandella of your Heart's Nature, "The Third Mary," progenitor of the Lady Mary Magdalene, speaker of Truth, Show-er of the Way and lover of the Light Within all Creation. And I am loving you, all of you, with a willing heart, forever and all-ways.

9/28/13

Good morning Dear One! I am Mo-Ray of the Archangelic Kingdom, "the Third Mary," Mother of the Lady Mary Magdalene, Speaker of Truth, Show-er of the Way, and Delineator of all Aspects of Consciousness that Carry the Light Forward Into Union. I have come today to suggest three things—Living Truthfully, as a mirror of one's own unique Divine Nature, Living Fully, as a member of the Planetary Re-memberance of Wholeness Within/Without, and Living Love's Full Freedom, in Oneness with All-that-Is.

The Lady Mary Magdalene took every opportunity to empower herself to be one with such experience. She lived her Truth most fully, as do I through your participation in my communication experience. She impacted many greatly and continues to do so through the ethers. She allowed herself to be used as a vehicle for many levels and dimensions of experience to express themselves here. When she walked through a forest, it knew her, and responded to her most meaningfully. She could call upon the forces of nature to assist her in her calling to partner with Jesus the Christ in helping humanity move toward Union. And she was very excited, thrilled even, to discover that she was the Keeper of the Grail, the living force that unites us all in our Love Nature.

This is not a golden cup, this is a bloodline that thirsts for Union beyond any and all other goals. Mary birthed three children through her Holy Union with Christ. This does not mean she had physical intercourse with him. This means that through her Sacred Union with him, their spiritual DNA ignited the Oneness factor so strongly that it was as if these children were born of the two of them. Their physical father was amazed at the similarities they bore to both spiritual parents. To see Jesus the Christ's face, or hair, or mannerisms in another one of his purported children could be a bit overwhelming sometimes, as if he were living a dream. My Mary bore two more after these three that lived full lives. There was one more, the last of her progeny, who was stillborn.

She had many happy memories of the youth of her daughters and sons. They spread throughout the globe to continue quietly, yet powerfully, continue building the momentum toward Union. They plan to make their identities known to the planet at the appropriate time, when this discovery will provoke the most joyous breakthrough. In the meantime, as I have done for so many eons as well, they are uniting their powers from the Unseen Realm with those who currently live and breathe upon the Earth plane.

I was able to meet one of the daughters, my granddaughter, just before my transition from the Earth plane. She was a beautiful thing, and recognized me right off. We had the same hairline and the same little dip in our noses. She took my hand and thanked me for everything I had done for my family, for her mother, the Lady Mary Magdalene, and for her personally, as she knew my Spirit had looked in on her and helped guide her at times. She told me her mother had shared with her everything I had taught her about the Goddess traditions, and that she spoke with great honoring of and longing towards me, a great love and respect. I was moved beyond words. This was perhaps the greatest single moment of this Earthly lifetime, which sometimes seemed longer than I cared for it to go on. I was very grateful to have lived to experience this day. And I knew it would be one of my last, for I felt my earthly connection, my physical life force energy, dwindling a little more each day.

It was a peaceful passing, attended by two of my sons and their daughters. I had lived well and done all I could to fulfill my purpose. I was complete in my time on the Earth in this form. And I knew great love through my sharing my calling toward Union and my time with Jesus the Christ and my daughter, the Lady Mary Magdalene, who exemplified this so well, beyond all probable odds and beyond the boundaries, the sense of limitation, that so often accompanies Earthly creation.

I am complete with this telling for now.

I remain, as always, Mo-Ray of the Archangelic Kingdom, Mary the Elder, the Mother of the Lady Mary Magdalene, Speaker of Truth, Show-er of the Way, and Live-er of Love's Full Flowering within and beyond all lifetimes. And I am loving you, all of you, completely, fully, forever and all-ways. And so it is.

9/29/13

Good morning, Dear One! I am Mo-Ray of the Archangelic Kingdom, the "Third Mary," Mother of the Lady Mary Magdalene, Speaker of Truth, Show-er of the Way. and Believer in the Good within the Hearts of All Humanity. I have come today to share with you my sutras, my "carry-forwards" of the Divine Nature's capabilities on the Earth Plane. Are you ready? *Yes.* Good.

1. **KNOW THYSELF!** I am aware this is not a new one, but there is no getting around it. It is imperative to have as comprehensive and accurate a sense of oneself on as many dimensions and timelines as conceivable in order to have as clear a concept of one's foundation and proclivities, inclinations, as possible. I am aware of this Truth's profound potential for attracting what most suits one into his or her life. And I am capable of trusting this ability to take you to new heights of awareness as yet unexplored, but extremely helpful in the Creation of Heaven on Earth.

2. **Assume nothing**. "Check into" everything by becoming more aware of its vibration, its energetic frequency. This is Truth, which cannot be faked or altered by any justification or disguise. The only *real* creations are those based in Truth. All else crumbles away in the Light, and the Light frequency is increasing exponentially *every day* upon the Earth plane now, hence the apparent mess that has built up over eons of miscreation is more and more visible and untenable, falling apart in this time of blazing Light streams. You are witnessing the dissolution of falsity, and the inner workings required for a firm foundation upon which the freedom for creating Heaven on Earth can be birthed, can be fully utilized. I am counting on the abilities of each one of you to live in this full freedom, this lack of falsehood each day, as we move forward into the Light together, in camaraderie and growth toward Union. I am facilitating your Highest Good manner of believing in yourself and your ability to make good on your Divine Birthright to seek and know Truth. And I am exploring those capabilities within you that help you uncover your own insights, accurately and fundamentally.

3. **Trust what your instincts are telling you** in each situation. Your body/mind/spirit has many ways of helping you to ignore outer forms of deception so you can recognize the Truth of how you are responding to all that is happening around you, whether or not

you are specifically aware of why you are responding this way. You do not have to "know" to trust! You may uncover this or not, it is okay. You do not have to justify your choice. If it is out of fear, or past association, or the following of some form of dogma or social credo, this will be made plain to you, so trust your instincts more and more and they will respond in kind by initiating you into ever greater levels of conscious awareness. You need no gurus to tell you so.

4. **Make yourself available to your inner world regularly.** This means a time-out from everyday activities, from outward action, so you can recognize and respond to inner awareness and connect more rapidly with your other-dimensional Light body and its calls to you. Your "teachers"—gurus, spirit guides and so on—are all sharing aspects of their frequencies as part of this Light body, which includes your Higher Self and Source connection. It radiates this spectrum of frequency in and around your body to one degree or another. Conscious awareness is key to more and more integration of these frequencies, such that all of the cells of your body, mind and being can radiate your Light more comprehensively and assist the catalyzation of your reality to express the experience of Heaven right here on Earth. That is what the Rainbow Bridge is for—living the fullness of Truth and Union ultimately found in human form through bridging the apparent gap between "high" and "low," "earthly" and acceptance, and absorption of the miracles of multi-dimensional reality.

I am recommending five to ten minutes of full immersion into your awareness of such inner realms daily for a fortnight, then increasing this length of time one to two more minutes a day for the next week or two, until you become ready to be more mindful of these multi-dimensional planes in your everyday world. I invite all of you to take the time to make space for more "inner reality" awareness.

Perhaps you have already completed a similar practice or perhaps have a similar daily routine. In this case, I/we recommend you substitute this "closed-eye" type of time with five minutes or so each day of sustained, "open-eyed" recognition of multidimensional reality. Ask to experience the Mind of God in your everyday reality, to see what your angels see, to recognize the Divine Union existing already upon the Earth plane. Open yourself to experience your reality in a fuller and more complete way. Perhaps you will assign a regular time each day, or have a signal to remind you to open to experience your world this way.

After a fortnight of following your inclinations for multi-sensory awareness consistently for a minimum of five minutes, more time is recommended, until you have reached fifteen to thirty minutes each day. You have now accomplished a great integration, and the day will come when you switch into this as your regular mode automatically as the planetary re-alignment locks in more comprehensively. In the meantime, allow yourself to explore this type of experience gradually. Do not try to force the integration process. This would actually move you away from more processing of the Light and into dis-reality and inaccuracy, inauthenticity, which would lead to great disruption in your personal life experience.

I am suggesting you play with the first version, the "closed-eye" version as a refresher before the "open-eyed" one if you have any doubts or concerns about the latter. You will find yourself switching over to it automatically if it is time for you to do so. If not, complete the first version, then take a pause of three days to a week, and then decide whether you prefer to continue with the new length of time for the closed-eye version, or if you truly feel good about exploring the open-eyed one.

I am not requiring *anyone* to do *anything* he or she does not already desire to do, because this is not a new reality for any of you. You *all* want more of it in your day-to-day world, even those who may seem to be frightened of it, for you are all made to desire Union and to experience Heaven on Earth. Else why so many sad songs and stories about *not* having a kind of experience like that? I can tell you that each one of these is expressing the desire for Union in the negative, in the "do-not-want-what I-have" form. And I can tell you that you are each intrinsically motivated to do your part in helping to move the Creation of Heaven on Earth along. I am relating this so you can better understand the changes occurring right now, and the capability within *each one of you* for greater and greater ease, flow and Grace in each choice, each moment of thought and activity, in your so-called "everyday" world. I am uniting this awareness, this level of frequency, to sustain each one of you more fully. And since I am one with you within the Unity of All Souls, we are *all* doing this *together!!!!!*

I am explaining these nuances not to justify, but to help you deliberately create a more conscious foundation for relating to the changes that are now occurring evolutionarily. And I am counting on *each one of you* to assist to the utmost possible for you in each moment.

If you are indeed living in the Truth of this "open-eyed" multi-dimensional reality daily, make sure you are fully grounded within the fiber of your being to the core frequency within planet earth, so you know you are fully connecting your physicality with this multi-dimensional reality. You might do so by "earthing," as they call it, most regularly, or by doing any practice that brings this palpably into your body/mind/spirit awareness. And I thank you for sharing your capabilities in this arena this far. It is very beneficial for all around you, and sustaining for your cells' nourishment, clarity and freedom of experiencing. You might notice some physical excretions that were not customary for you as you acclimate to your new level of multi-dimensional reality awareness, but it will not be of any great intensity or duration for you, simply a bit of residual internal clearing, moving external attributes to reach a new plateau of cleansing.

I am remarking upon this only because there are those of you who believe they must suffer in some way to reach those new heights. Some shift is unavoidable, but it need not lead to the degree of disruption you have imagined or been a party to before. And I am enjoying your ability to say "yes" to more of what delights you, as you assist yourself to live more fully in the Light of Truth each day. I am aware of your ability to include multi-dimensional reality more rapidly now into your awareness, and it is *extremely* satisfying to know you are going to live it quite soon upon the Earth plane. I can almost taste it for you, but not quite!

And I am aware of your ability to open your heart and throat chakras more, those vital energy centers for hearing, speaking and being truth that so many of you had shut down in the past, such that you can know this aspect of yourself more completely now. I am expecting all the best for each one of you in this regard, because the time is coming for *all* to be upheld in the Divine Union that is our birthright. And I am appreciating the power of this expectancy to assist you in recognizing this knowing within yourself now.

5. **Eliminate your prior delusions about your smallness** by recognizing the greatness within the core of who you are, and *release* all external reminders you have carried about such. Allow them to be shifted into reflections of who you are, into aspects of stories of wholeness, or *let them go!!!!!!!!!* I think you are aware by now of the power of shaping your physical reality to express your Divine Nature and the sense of limitation that cannot be admissible in creating Heaven On Earth, so *release* your hold on these artifacts of delusion. *Let them go!!!!!!!*

6. **Insist upon acknowledging the wealth of experience, the deliberate creation of positive outcome in your world.** See, hear, know how much good is occurring, and express your delight and appreciation for

such most clearly. Use your creativity to allow yourself more freedom to play, to explore, in this area. And just know that this is vital also to creating the Union experience of Heaven on Earth. As you persist in such acknowledgment, you will ground this appreciation into your being in such a way that *all* will vibrate more fully to this Truth.

7. **Be available to your Higher Knowing more consistently by <u>writing it down</u>!!!** I cannot emphasize this enough. It will help you in more ways and on more levels than you recognize consciously. It truly assists you in doing your part to live in Oneness, in Divine Union and *all else* will assimilate it in your world. I am allowing you to recognize your own worth more fully by explaining to you the power of *your* knowing to be integrated more fully into your everyday consciousness world by inscribing it physically. You are your own guru, as you are part of every and all energies that ever were, are and will be, so go for it!!!!

Whenever you doubt the truth of what you are inscribing, just put it away for three weeks; then pull it out again and notice how it feels. Are you recognizing the power of your penning this down now? Are you willing to experience what has been related through you? Or are you noticing residual doubt and distrust? Is this warranted? Do you have the Keys to Truth more fully tucked away than you had previously imagined? Pray for guidance on this if it is still unclear to you. And do your utmost to have your neutrality revealed to you.

8. **Justify your new level of heightened reality to no one, including yourself.** Simply accept and allow it as your new norm. It shall feel even better than you currently imagine. Know you are more than worthy to allow yourself a full and complete relationship with the Divinity of your Life experience and all of the wealth it shall accrue.

9. **Whenever you remove yourself from a so-called negative, insist upon exploring the value you have released by doing so,** including the many resulting creations/positive influences and effects of this, so *you* are steeped in the wealth and nuances of this experiences' up side.

This is enough for now. I thank you for your diligence in scribing all this down at this time and please know I am greatly available to you in each moment.

I remain, as always, Mo-Ray of the Archangelic Kingdom, the "Third Mary," Mother of the Lady Mary Magdalene, Speaker of Truth, Show-er of the Way, and Uniter of Apparent Opposites in the Fullness of Divine Union through Non-Local Awareness. And I am loving each and every one of you, forever and all-ways.

10/6/13

Good morning, Dear Heart! I am Mo-Ray of the Archangelic Kingdom, the "Third Mary," Mother of the Lady Mary Magdalene, Speaker of Truth, Show-er of the Way and a Keeper of the Flame Within the Hearts of All Humanity, the Light Core that Sustains and Feeds Us, without which we could not exist. I have come today to share with you much of the reason behind your current turmoil, your current unrest.

It is the Awakening, and its friction with that which requires refinement to serve the greater whole. It is without a doubt the single greatest occurrence on Earth to be part of the larger continuum of evolution happening throughout the greater cosmos and it behooves *all of you* to do your best to "get on board," so to speak. What I mean is to ask yourself every day, "What do I *truly* desire? What do I value most? What would I not want to be here without?" And honor the *essence,* the *core* of your responses, to the best of your ability in each moment. I am trying to assist you in carrying this forth by reminding you of your worth, your true value, and the importance of clarifying and acting upon your real priorities as opposed to any illusion you were taught to consider such.

I am remarkable for my insistence upon this, although I too was in many ways trained to put societal priorities first as well. I can tell you that this shift is *the* shift required for personal *and planetary* fulfillment, and that each one of you who carries this through, who pierces the veil of inequity, shall arrive in the true Promised Land and revel in this change. It is indeed of epic proportions. You yourself are three-quarters of the way through this process. There is more yet to go. And it is all good. Every step along this path is a valuable one, increasing exponentially with each passage through the next doorway, tunnel, and fork in the road. When you "arrive," you will recognize all that you desire most fully, greeting you with joy and elation, for you, each one of you, will *truly* know yourself as cherished, cherishable, and truly at home here. It is not a *location,* it is a situation, one we have been building toward for eons. And you, each one of you, has the key to, the knowing of, how to bring yourself here within you. The Kingdom is within. You know how to arrive. Simply take the next step before you. Trust your own innate honing ability to get you there. You will unfold gloriously through your process, and benefit *multitudes* through your experience. Your action multiplies the capacity for others to take their *own* initiative and facilitates their way by bringing more ease, more flow, more Grace of lubrication, as it were, to the turning of the wheel of their processes.

I am escalating your reminders because the greater continuum's alignment with the creation of Heaven on Earth is growing stronger each moment. You cannot delay without experiencing greater friction in your everyday world. And I am all for the gloriousness of Greater Joy, Grace, and Ease in this world of yours. So I am reminding you once again to DREAM BIG, recognize your true value, act upon your ultimate goals in each moment to the best of your ability, (which may often be attitudinal), and trust your own process for your own road to creating Heaven on Earth. It begins within and creates without. And I am truly grateful for every bit, every morsel of your creation of it. For you, each one of you, share aspects of my own heart. And you, each one of you, deserves full respect and glory, for your soul is Heaven-blessed and chosen to be a part of this spectacular Earth time. And I am proud of each one of you for your ability to become a part of the Peace of a Million Years Dreaming, to bridge the gap that has seemed to exist between the Heavens and the Earth plane.

This is enough for now. I share my love with each one of you. Call upon me often, for I am Mo-Ray of the Archangelic Kingdom, the "Third Mary," Mother of the Lady Mary Magdalene, Mirandella of your heart, your soothing place, Speaker of Truth, Show-er of the Way, and Keeper of the Records of the Points of Light Within All Earthly Creation and beyond. And I am loving you, each one of you, forever and all-ways.

10/7/13

Good day, Dear One! I am Mo-Ray of the Archangelic Kingdom, the "Third Mary," Mother of Lady Mary Magdalene, Speaker of Truth, Show-er of the Way and Delineator of All Helpful Aspects of Consciousness for Sharing the Light Rays. I have come today to assist you with your qualities that help you create fulfillment in your world. I am expecting great things, great *experiences*, for each one of you. And you can coax them forth through anticipating and participating in greater personal growth, the kind that envelops every aspect of your being and changes your viewpoint vastly to include larger and larger units of experience and whole-life perspective. I have initiated each one of you reading these words scribed into my venture of plenitude through your souls' agreement with that of my own, and we can investigate together the winds of evolution that are transforming your lives and worlds. When you reread our words, you will know better how to harmonize with these shifts at will. For now, utilize your capacity for adventure to assist yourself to imagine your life as it will be when the final harmonization of this evolutionary phase is complete. I can you tell you it shall be greater than this, but your imagination is a powerful bridge to utilize in the interim. And I *know* you can feel these harmonic nuances within your own vibrational territory whenever you bring your attention to them. Tune in to their abilities whenever you are willing to allow yourself to *feel* them more fully. After a while, you will notice subtle changes in your experience of the world around you and your opinions of its substance. What matters, what counts to you, will lean toward greater harmonious liberation of thought, feeling and action as you begin to utilize this expansion more and more frequently, and with greater adeptness.

Because I have anticipated traveling this road with you many times before, for eons I have worked with adepts at positive change creation within your galaxy and beyond. Many frequencies are available to help you utilize your own innate capacities and awareness more fully now, and I can assist you in connecting with them if you so choose. Simply call upon me whenever you feel moved to do so. Open to translate the frequencies available to you into thought, sound, word, idea, if you choose, by focusing upon your knowing that it is your nature to do so, and allow the rest to unfold. Each of you will have different experiences, different methods for attuning with those off-world frequencies that I have indicated as beneficial to you. When you remove your barriers to fulfillment, it is complete. Your energetic frequency will begin to absorb and create all that you desire to transpire. And your willingness to do so abounds now.

So ask yourself, "What do I truly desire now?" And allow your core responses to unfold. I will assist you most readily upon completion of your soul-to-soul advisement with me. And you may rest assured that all is developing rapidly on the etheric plane as we all approach the continuity of experience that welcomes Heaven's advancement into Earthly Creation.

I am enjoying your growth every bit as fully as your own soul's guiding consciousness, and can tell you that everything you've truly hoped for lies just around the corner for you. And I am willing to bet that as you function more deliberately through your powers of creation, your energetic discharge, or byproduct, as it were, will elevate many who came by your greatness for upliftment ingenuously, for it is the ripples that can heal your world ***profoundly.***

So, I will leave off this topic for now and remind you that I am capable and willing to speak to you of other things, all in due course and timing. I am aware that your nature requires you to indulge in more examples of things, more "concrete" realities, and I am assisting you in correlating these with the untold aspects of my realm and nature, so you will better understand and appreciate their significance for you and all. I can allow every part of me to be woven into your conscious awareness through my energetic expression of beingness, so my nature can impart to you its relevance to your own experience and world. And I am trusting your own capacity for spiritual adeptness to correlate with my own, such that we may weave greater and greater tapestries of energetic expression into your Earthly realm.

And so for now, I bid you adieu.

I remain, as always, Mo-Ray of the Archangelic Kingdom, the Third Mary, Mother of the Lady Mary Magdalene, Speaker of Truth, Show-er of the Way, and Builder of Unique Frequency Expressions of Infinite Consciousness-Raising. And I am loving all of you, forever and all-ways.

10/8/13

Good morning, Dear One! I am Mo-Ray of the Archangelic Kingdom, the Third Mary at Truth's Door, Vibrating Realities for all Beings Who Choose Heaven for Earth, Mother of the Lady Mary Magdalene, Mirandella of Your Heart, Speaker of Truth, Show-er of the Way, and Repeater of Essence Views for ALL Who Hear Love's VOICE.

I have come today to accept your choice to be more fully alive on the Earth Plane, on behalf of the Council of Light and as a true representative of your soul's calling. I am your advanced aspect's true voice, speaking to you through the ethers in such a way that you might vibrate more fully to it, more completely embody it, and more profoundly live it! I have come to facilitate your movement, your growth in this manner. And I am layering your awareness with stories of all worlds—past, present, future, simultaneously. Whenever you reveal essence, you bring your awareness to "non-local reality," that which is beyond time and space, though you may navigate from it. I leave you truths that are branches of one tree—the Tree of Life/Love/Freedom of True Beingness, at-one with, and for being with, WHO YOU ARE AT YOUR CORE, your essence, your Life Stream of Living Love, your slice of *REALITY*, YOUR GOD NATURE! I exude awareness of this because I have chosen to develop this skill vibrationally over many, many lifetimes and beyond. I train and develop in the Unseen, and gift you through the stars to awaken your vibrational fullness, to help you to complete your mission, your chosen purpose, and your mode of being in every lifetime in which you choose my nature. I support your process of *Self* recognition and assist you to vibrate more fully to it, to attune to it more precisely, and to envision your mastery of total Self expression.

I am willing to play this role because my own development came so powerfully through my raising of the young Lady Mary Magdalene, who lived her shining Truth so completely. It was even more of a rarity then and there than in your world. And of course, the Christed One did this as well.

I have chosen, you have chosen, to make my calling more palpable in your time and place than previously because now is the time for all doors to be opened, for All Truth to be revealed, and for all who hunger for real transformation to experience it, as we evolve our Heavenly Nature into a more fully integrated Earth plane experience, the Living and Loving in Heaven on Earth.

I am told you are experiencing more juice, more substance in your everyday world. This signals to me that you are deliberately knowing and expressing your Self more completely than ever before and that you are mastering new aspects of your own vibration. It is good.

I am exceptionally proud of all you choose to enlighten yourself with, including your choice of friendships and way of upholding them, as you maneuver into greater and greater fullness of your unique expression.

When you exhibit more of who you really are, you become more available to unfolding aspects of your Soul's nature that you were less conscious of before, and this is part of the great evolution now occurring. Whenever you sample new aspects of your core value, you widen your approach to choosing Heaven for Earth, and increase your ability to help facilitate its creation. When you dig in to the soul's vibration, the harmonies forthcoming tune themselves to your experience for transformation and require new avenues, new thoughts, for enlivening your experience. I chose my "work" to display a vibrational pull, my deep yearning for realizing Divine Nature here, now, because I am an aspect of yourself that chooses the Living Love frequency. I am heard because you are tuned in to this vibration, because you are choosing to be this with me now, because you are of that which I am sourced from as well, and which indeed all are—we are of the Creator and that shall always be.

What changes in your consciousness is your willingness to allow that which you are sourced from to be available for you, and embodied by you, in all times and throughout all situations! For you to be able to express me now, to hear what I have to tell you, means you have recognized and embodied enough of your Soul nature to be capable of this and to utilize your existence more fully in service to this ability in all others. Else why even bother?

We are all one at the core in Truth, yet we allow our ability to assimilate ourselves into greater recognition of our Union, Our Oneness, our wholeness together, to devolve into experiences of lack and/or limitation, of separateness and dis-allowal of the aforementioned vibrational reality. Whenever we are called to act upon our knowing of Truth, it is good, whether we feel we are up to it or not. I am telling you this because many consider it a sign of troubles to come when they are asked, when they feel vibrationally compelled, to make a change, a shift, that might allow them to become more available to the Truth of whom they really are, to the Truth of Divine Union, of Wholeness, within Earth's time/space reality. You are unique to your kind, each one of you, as you navigate through the pools, through the tides, through the waters that cleanse you and motivate you to change, to reveal with more clarity your own Divine Nature.

I am sharing all of this detail with you so you may find your way to ever greater experiences of clarity, of Soul-filled living and Oneness with your own Divine Nature. And I am calling you forward because that is my own Truth, that is what I am available for.

I am giving these teachings through you now so you may support this process in yourself and all others more completely and naturally. I can observe the changes within you closely and assist you vibrationally to achieve your soul's desires within the Earth plane temple, the vehicle you have chosen for embodiment in your time/space reality. I am wondering when you exhibit signs of fatigue, whether you are truly tired or whether you are creating an experience of such based on distrust of your own capabilities for fruitful living. Perhaps you are inviting a sense of disengagement with what is happening around you, a lack of involvement in the situation, or even a negative response to it. This in itself creates a misunderstanding of the energies present, devolving into a sense of disharmony that creates an experience of fatigue in you.

This is not to suggest there is no actual, physical fatigue to experience, or that you should not listen to and allow for your body/mind/spirit needs for fulfillment through resting time, simply that more attention may be paid to the true cause of the experience, so you might disentangle yourself from unrequired lackfulness, and avail yourself of more opportunities for wholeness and Divine Self expression.

When you are feeling fatigued, ask yourself, "Is this of my body/mind/spirit? Or is this of my lack of interest or negativity toward what is now happening around me? If it be the latter, how might I experience this anew, or extricate myself from such more consciously, without relying upon a notion of physical fatigue as a requirement?"

I am sure each one of you has recognized boredom in yourself when exposed to situations in which you've disallowed your natural harmony as a response to that which does not ignite your enthusiasm, valuing or respect. Yet you have available to you in all moments ways to view this differently and/or allow yourself to disengage, to leave the situation, while respecting the desires, the interests and enthusiasms of others. This wisdom keeps you connected through your awareness with these others, while allowing you to express your own aspects of your Divine Nature with integrity. I am suggesting you explore avenues for growth in this because you are all exposed to what does not fully excite you more frequently these days, as part of the movement toward Union. Still, it does not mean you can and do respect all the outer doings of humankind, but that you live love and focus upon the expression of core nature that is within each and every one, and uncover that Unity through your thought processes and Divine awareness, so you may invite more experiences of this Unity to play out in your world, and receive the joy available to you as a witness thereof.

I am grateful you are willing to bear through my detailed analysis of this, because I can be more helpful, more assistive to others in this manner. I am True Availability to Your Own Soul Beingness come to call upon you, to open a door to greater Freedom/Wholeness/Truth/Order/Union/Fulfillment because this is WHO I AM!!!! I invite you to call upon me at any time and I will assist greatly.

If you doubt our ability to create in this way together, recognize that we already have been through your experience of reading this book, and, as the one scribing this can relate, it is more than the sounds of the words themselves, more than the surface of their meanings, more than can be ignored vibrationally. You are participating with me in moving beyond the Grand Illusion and into the Oneness, the Unity, the Receiving of the Creation of Heaven on Earth.

And so it is.

I remain, as always, your unique translator of Beingness, your Heaven-On-Earth door holder. I am Mo-Ray of the Archangelic Kingdom, Mirandella of Your Heart, the Third Mary, Mother of the Lady Mary Magdalene, Speaker of Truth, Show-er of the Way, and Detailer of Aspects of Creating Unity Consciousness Within and Throughout Planet Earth and Beyond. And I am loving each one of you, forever and all-ways.

10/9/13

Good morning, Dear One! I am the Third Mary of the Triumvirate for Peace, Hope and Grace, also known to you as Mo-Ray of the Archangelic Kingdom, Mirandella of Your Heart. I am the Mother of the Lady Mary Magdalene, Speaker of Truth, Show-er of the Way, and Translator of Many Useful Frequencies in Your World. I have come today to clarify for you many things regarding Christ's birth, the Lady Mary Magdalene's role, and their subsequent choices and outcomes.

When I was a very young girl, an elder of our coven took me aside and spoke to me quite plainly of everything my soul had chosen regarding my current lifetime while in the Swing between Worlds. She was reminding me of all that was locked somewhere in my awareness, so I would be strengthened in my resolve to prepare well for these changes. I became a very self-motivated learner of our Goddess traditions and quietly self-taught in some additional, related practices, all to strengthen me for the times to come, and to assist me in the upbringing of the Lady Mary Magdalene. And it went well for me in this regard. I took to those processes and rituals quite naturally and began to explore my own co-creation with nature bit by bit, until I understood the groundwork from which Jesus the Christ and the Lady Mary Magdalene would help to create many miracles.

I knew Mary, Jesus's mother, from my dreams first, and also dim memories of our times together in the Swing Between the Worlds. She was a Shining One too. She foretold her role through the eons to me both in dreams and in private moments in person. She recognized me as well. I will never forget her beautiful smile when we first met in person. The smell of roses was subtly with her even then, and she knew I had recognized her too. We embraced and experienced one another's soul nature even more strongly. She truly is a Queen of Heaven beyond that which any words can describe, and I would have willingly laid down my life for hers at any moment had this been necessary, even with my purpose of training the Lady Mary Magdalene, for I knew she could fill that role too, if required. Neither of us was yet pregnant with our girls. I had just the one young son as yet. It was a "chance" encounter. She was with a nomadic group, staying at an encampment nearby. We met at the waters. She told me she would return again when her foretold son was three years old, that he might meet my Mary.

And it was good. I felt warmed, comforted by her presence and the ability to share our knowings. In the years that followed, I felt her essence come to me many times, and it always reassured me. Sometimes she reminded me of who I was and why I'd come here, when I felt tired or forlorn, for she knew the travails of a young mother, and the lack of freedoms required in our world and society. She knew the challenges involved in both of our choices, and her sweet nature soothed my own most profoundly even just to think of her. Jesus's mother was, and is, a true piece of heaven, and I am most grateful to have known her in this lifetime.

When Jesus was three years old and my Mary almost five, they met and played together. It was a wondrous delight to see them together and witness their joy and playfulness. We regretted they could not be together more often, but we understood the reasons for all this, both internally and socially. Whenever they were together, all of Life shone more brightly around. They radiated their souls' energy so profoundly that the air around them was quite charged, and everything seemed more alive and youthful. Those were special times. We did our best, the other Mary and I, to cloak their privacy from others, that they might have this freedom, this joy of being together, for its own right and to help sustain them in the future. It might have helped them trust their togetherness too, when illusions of separation were presented to them.

But all that was in the future. In this time, their elation in playing together fed our own souls mightily. Whenever I remember those times, I feel that youthful vibrancy and aliveness, that crashing of souls together in glorious frequencies, the magnificence of their purest love. Those were grand experiences that continue to resound across the ages.

The young Jesus would have the most mischievous little grin on his face at times, and whenever he saw me grow serious, he would give me that look and I would return to the delight of the moment. He knew I could be overwhelmed at times, and even as a young boy, he would take my hand, or touch my hair, or give me that little smile, and my cares would go.

I trusted Jesus the Christ as no man other than Judas Iscariot to play out fully his chosen role. I knew him deeply, and would willingly have laid down my life for him as well, had it been possible and helpful to our cause, our roles in helping to create Union/Heaven on Earth.

I will tell you this—Jesus was a handsome young man and there was not a little girl who wouldn't have given her all for one of his famous smiles. He was kind to everyone, but there was no one whose presence lit him up like our Young Mary. And I know she was completely taken with him as well. Whenever these two were together, it was a glory.

I know you have more questions around their relationship, and I promise you, they will be answered in due course. For now, it is time for you to get on with your day.

I remain, as always, the Third Mary of the Triumvirate for Peace, Hope and Grace, Mother of the Lady Mary Magdalene, Speaker of Truth, Show-er of the Way and Translator of Many Wonderful Frequencies that Resound Throughout Your World and beyond. And I am loving you, *all* of you, forever and all-ways!!!!

🕊 THE THIRD MARY

10/10/13

Good morning, Dear One! I am the Third Mary of the Triumvirate of Peace, Hope and Grace, Mother of the Lady Mary Magdalene, Speaker of Truth, Show-er of the Way. I am also known as Mo-Ray of the Archangels, and Mirandella of Your Heart. I have come today to assist you in better understanding your own heart and its antecedents from prior lifetimes, particularly those of biblical times. I support your understanding through my energetic infrastructure and its link-up with your own. I am explaining these relationships in a more general way to allow for individual means of expression to come forth. You each have your own sort of inner vocabulary for making sense of such things and I want you to explore through feeling for your own way of understanding this. I am gentle, strong and clear in helping you develop your own awareness of Truth and Union, so you may empower yourself more effectively. I am sure you may trust your inner world more than you currently do, and you can continue to develop your gifts much more rapidly once you do so.

I am willing to pick up the pace now on sharing my perspective on the true meaning of Jesus the Christ and the Lady Mary Magdalene's roles and their outcomes in this lifetime.

When young Mary was six years old, she told me everything she knew of her story, so she would know on every level that we both carried this Truth in our hearts and souls. She told me of her memories of the Swing Between the Worlds, of the choices she had and would make to assist the Christ through Oneness and Union of purpose. She foretold the timing of her death, the births of her Spirit children with Christ, and other key moments of her lifetime. She told me this one winter's night when all the others were fast asleep and we were still sitting together. She knew I would remind her with my eyes if ever it looked as if she had forgotten. She was a very unusual child.

When she was fourteen years old, she told me she would be going away soon, to study privately so she might be better prepared for the time of the Quickening of Christ's role. I wished her well and made it appear to all that she was going to help a cousin who had recently borne her third child. She returned six months later with the strength and confidence of a young woman, and continued her blossoming each day.

It was difficult at times for her to assume so many roles at once, for she was a governess to many young children in our area, a teacher to little ones, a member of our coven, a budding healer, and an assistant in our household, all while having an inner world in which she communed with the young Jesus and ran her energy with aspects of the natural world. I often wondered how she could facilitate so much at once, but when I remembered the circumstances of her birth and her powerful nature, I understood.

Even so, there were times when she just needed a break, a time to run off to the river where she and the young Jesus had played when little, to refresh herself and just be. At such times, I would run what interference I could. I often had Martha fill in for her in those ways she could at such times. As I have mentioned, Martha could be a stubborn child and quite petulant, but she was also proud to be able to fill in for her older sister in some regards within the household and with the small children. She was aware that Mary's faculties were sometimes stretched to the limit, though she was unaware of all the reasons for this. Fortuitously, she often assisted with Judas's young brother's care when he was quite young, helping to connect our families further. And she could hold her own in any conversation involving the matching of wits, for she could be quite a debater!

When Jesus the Christ was fully blossomed, Martha was quite taken with him. She would have done anything to be by his side, were this possible. Her longing was so great at times I wondered whether it would split our home apart, and at a certain point, emotionally, it did. She was a headstrong young woman, wanting her way in all things. When Jesus came into the room, she would put everything on hold to be with him. It was very plain to all just how possessive of him she would like to be, including to her sister Mary. And though Jesus was remarkably kind to her, it was just as plain that she held no special personal place in his heart the way Mary did. It was Mary Jesus came to privately and spoke with late into the night, Mary whom he connected with from any part of a room, and Mary who sang to him when he desired respite. She lit him up, and he her, on every level. Though Mary tried to speak with young Martha about this triangulation, it was no use. She would not believe the truths Mary tried to explain to her, for she wanted to believe herself an equal competitor for Jesus's hand and refused to recognize the honesty and compassion with which Mary approached her, distrusting her and feeling all the more venom toward her.

These were tense times for me, knowing also the time was coming for the main stage performances of our story's key players. All who were part of this had increasing concern for their abilities to fulfill their souls' responsibilities to their choices. I myself often wondered whether I would have the strength to let my daughter go when the time came, and whether I had done enough to help prepare her for her challenges. Indeed, there were so many levels of stories and truth to be played out, such that would resound across the eons and galaxies. We each had our times of stress and our times of knowing. Fortunately, none of us hit our lows at the same moments and our connections held strong such that each became a buoy and a life rope to the other. It was also our good fortune that we had pre-arranged signals to use for times of great distress. This prescience served us well and facilitated much required assistance.

I know this may all sound a bit conspiracy-like and it's true. It was a conspiracy of thought, word and deed, designed on the Highest Order and for the Highest purpose that we could claim—the moving forward of the Creation of Heaven on Earth.

I have much more to say on this topic; however, I will leave you with this for now—I recognized Martha's inability to be trusted, so I recommended, after great forethought and consultation in the Inner Realms, that her nature be put to use in the advancement of our work. This was not pre-ordained during our time in the Swing Between the Worlds, so I was very cautious in considering how this all might play out. She was not used, in the sense of being regarded simply as a means to an end. She was just given opportunities for growth beyond her present status that could serve both herself and the larger whole through our pictured outcomes of events. And she came through marvelously, eventually, though as I have said, it took her many Earth years to complete this.

This is enough for now. It behooves you to get on with the rest of your day.

I remain, as always, the Third Mary of the Triumvirate of Peace, Hope and Grace for the New Millennia, the Mother of the Lady Mary Magdalene, Mirandella of Your Heart, and Mo-Ray of the Archangelic Kingdom. I am a Speaker of Truth and Show-er of the Way in my own right, as was the daughter of my soul, the Lady Mary Magdalene. And I am loving you, forever and all-ways!!!!

THE THIRD MARY

10/11/13

Good morning, Dear One! I am Mo-Ray of the Archangelic Kingdom, the Third Mary of the Triumvirate for Creating Heaven on Earth, Mother of the Lady Mary Magdalene, Speaker of Truth, Show-er of the Way, and Explainer of Many Aspects of Earth's Descent through the Heavens. I have come today to tell you more about biblical times, more truths to absorb, more turmoils to absolve, more miracles to enlighten. I was very fortunate to have a very close, as well as a bird's eye view of the topic at hand. And then again, I was well-trained to do so. And it was miracle after miracle that created Jesus the Christ's story, and Mary Magdalene's role as his trusted counterpart.

They were inseparable at this point—he the Speaker, the Awakener of Consciousness through the Sound of his voice, the touch of his hand, the presence of his being. All of Heaven and Earth flowed together in support. And Mary was an invaluable transducer of these energies, assisting the Christ through telekinesis and various energetic translations to be fully present and available to others as his Christed Self, appointed to wake up the awareness of all to the possibilities of Heaven on Earth. He was a powerful transmitter of the energies who required a counterpart on the Earth Plane to hold the magnitude, the intensity of this energetic presence within him. Jesus was, and is, a son of God who presenced total Union with his Heavenly aspect. It was foretold that he would undergo great trials in sharing this, and that he would never lose his resolve to do so, in spite of these. For he had much to accomplish in his Earthly lifetime, and he knew it.

Mary would come to him, after the long, hot days, the many crowds, the speaking in parables, and be his succor, his healer. She helped him to release the energetic holds that others attempted to place upon him, and to rest profoundly. She shared his supper with him, (quite unusual in those days and times), held his feet, shared the love in her eyes, gave him respite. She knew more than any of the others what made him tick and what gave him respite. He was a tall order to meet, and meet him she did. When he was with the crowds, she spoke quietly to onlookers who ventured outside the edges, gave them the opportunity to see how this might appear through her eyes. She kept a watch on things overall, lent her keen mind to Jesus the Christ's goals, her whole heart and soul. She radiated loving presence and helped heal many who came to their door. Jesus was the outward and she the inward at this time of their partnering. And it was understood that she was the closest of everyone to him within our inner circle. It was out of love for humanity and its potential that they chose to accomplish all they did.

Could Jesus the Christ have done all he did without the Lady Mary Magdalene, you ask? He was *never* dependent on her. They were interdependent at this time. It was a true Union of equal souls, counterbalancing and co-creating their work together. Everyone who came into contact with one was assisted by the other, whether they knew it or not. And everyone was charged with levels of being that would not have been as coherent, as consistent, as relatable, as readily, gracefully and fully absorbed, without the energetic partnership of these two with their Creator. Male and female aspects of both created a profound fusion that assisted in ways beyond words. Even I am at a loss to describe such magnificence.

And it would behoove each one of you to understand that you too may help with this project. You too carry energetic rays to be found identically nowhere else. You too have special keys to the creating of Heaven On Earth. You too have a Divine Appointment calling to you. And you too have a counterpart without which your mission cannot be as flowingly accomplished, be it male or female, embodied on the Earth plane or connecting through the Unseen, be it a "love" relationship, sibling, parent-child, or friend, there is someone who can help you to grow and accomplish your mission more fully, someone who is bringing valuable codes for your part in the creation of Heaven on Earth, someone who can bring forth certain aspects that are powerfully assistive. Unite with your goal and you unite with this being. And vice versa. You do not have to know this one's identity or understand how this can occur for it to happen. You will undergo many rapid changes in the next few months and years. In that time, you will become more aware of energetic frequencies that have been hidden from you for eons. You will empower yourself greatly through understanding that *YOU*, without exception, are the Deliverance of Unification throughout your world. You are the power to create Heaven's entry here. You are unmasked to reveal the Divinity possible here on the Earth Plane. You are absolved of your past errors, you are being cleansed of all residue remaining of "karma." You are unfolding rapidly and magnificently. You are coming into full blossom now. And you are sharing energetic frequencies with your counterpart in ways that strengthen and uphold this process.

You are in groups of twenty-four souls that work this energetic coherence more interactively. Some call this your soul group. You are not always in the same outward field or career/similar means of expression, but you all cohere, have a certain core resonance with specific energetic structures, and play off one another's spark grandly.

You do not have to understand any of this to begin. Just know that you are creating vital assistance to particular others in moving their specific purpose forward and vice versa, and that the more you align with the magnitude of your Inner Being and its value, its strength and calling, the more fully you will experience what I have described.

It may help you to know I was not aware of this pull to unification through the assistance of another 'til I had time to absorb fully the story of Jesus the Christ and Mary's partnership after they had gone. I was not available for conscious appreciation of this in my personal world, for I was caught up in the events of the time and their own magnitude. There was much for me to sort upon their leaving, and my own healing had just begun from certain aspects of consciousness that were foreign to my nature and impinged upon it. I was weak at times, despite my holding up enough of my end of the bargain. I allowed myself to feel abused, though this was of no benefit to my being. I understand the willingness to undergo hardship to achieve a greater goal, and the vulnerability, the potential to focus on the hardship in and of itself at times. I was a wounded healer for a time. I recommend laying your heart open to your Creator if you feel this describes you as well, and asking directly for assistance. It will come to you in many forms, discreetly at times, overtly at others.

I am caring for you and sharing my heart with you most fully, for I know you are creating as best you know how, that you are striving for a purpose, and you are willing to call upon Heaven as Earth to assist you to carry through your part in its creation. I am understanding of the kind of woes and cares many of you carry, and that much can be washed away, released, if you allow yourself to open to the miracles that abound, that are happening, and that are being energetically prepared in the interim. For all is in readiness for you to emerge into your full glory as we carry the momentum for the Creation of Heaven on Earth forward.

I love you truly, forever and all-ways. I am Mo-Ray of the Archangelic Kingdom, the Third Mary of the Triumvirate for the Creation of Heaven on Earth, Mother of the Lady Mary Magdalene, Speaker of Truth, Show-er of the Way, and I am very proud of you, all of you, for being willing to be here, and to be who you are so profoundly in this time and place. I am with you. You may call upon me at any time. And I am willing to hear *your* story. I remain indebted to you for allowing yourself to be so useful here, Dear One. And I am willing to continue to share these Bible time stories with you on the morrow. Au revoir.

10/12/13

Good morning, Dear One! I am Mo-Ray of the Archangelic Kingdom, the Third Mary of the Triumvirate for the Creation of Heaven on Earth, Mother of the Lady Mary Magdalene, Speaker of Truth, Show-er of the Way, Mirandella of Your Heart. I have come today to tell you of the changing times of way back when, the biblical times and beyond. I am sure you have wondered many things about the truth or inaccuracy of what you've been told by both myself and others. I know it is difficult to understand what is not concrete for you, what implies life beyond living, what increases your puzzlement because it shifts other awarenesses in your mind. I can tell you there is much to absorb from any story of value, any trait of awareness, and any wonder you may experience. The life and times of Jesus the Christ and the Lady Mary Magdalene are packed with much of these attributes, and continue to charge and activate key players in the creating of Heaven on Earth. There are many layers to explore, many aspects to define, many energy waves to unpackage, unfold, set free to empower you in this world.

My story is not for everyone's awareness. My story is for those who choose to hear it. My story is for those whose desire for Heaven on Earth is a natural force lifting them to new planes of experience. My story is for those who understand that a mother's heart is valuable, has worth, is necessary in the unfolding awareness of portions of Jesus the Christ's and the Lady Mary Magdalene's story. My story is for those who desire absolution from earthly woes and are willing to shift their own energetic frequencies to support this. My story is for everyone who desires to be at his or her full potential. My story is meant to awaken you to your own significance through deepening your awareness of the truth of those biblical times and by activating your own abilities more strongly for assisting in the Creation of Heaven on Earth.

My story is for those of you who are tired of the same old pendulum swing of duality, who want to experience Heaven as Earth NOW, who enjoy listening within for their Truth signal.

My story is for all ages and times. My story is encompassing, weaving through and protecting your story. My story is about the giving and receiving of love on all levels. My story is without end, for it is of the Infinite. My story rests within your story, as you unfold your own gifts and nature wisely. My story accrues its wisdom through the compilation and interweaving of all stories of reclamation inviting personal truth to come together with the Absolute and Eternal.

My story is simply one story with many wings to impart truth through many angles of perambulation. And it is trying to speak through your story in such a way that it might uplift, sustain and empower you to tell the power of your own inner world's story, and to keep you engaged with your Higher Nature throughout your time here on Earth.

My story is unveiled through your willingness to discern it as just a piece of the larger puzzle of creating Heaven on Earth. My story is to impart to you the meaning, the significance that will grow your awareness more fully in these new times through new awareness of the meaning, the significance, of the old times.

My story is my story, available to accept or reject as you please. But it cannot leave you untouched, unmoved, unchanged, because it begins with your piece of the puzzle for creating Heaven on Earth in it. And it is multi-layered with energies for your Highest Good.

My story is helpful for those who choose to live their lives more fully, as sentient creatures on Heaven as Earth, and to remind you of your own Divine Nature.

My story is willing to support your story in shining Truth's Light over all creation, and to support the growth of Light here for all.

My story is a doorway for all who choose to enter. Let us enter together now.

When Jesus and Mary held their hands together, they imparted many frequencies throughout the Universe. They were supported by the Nature Kingdoms and protected by the Archangels. They were driven to fulfill their public roles more prominently. When Jesus gave his Sermon on the Mount, he and Mary had already foresworn their Love and Unity to one another, and this mighty pact, this spiritual ceremony, bore fruit most rapidly. She was a beautiful creature, who turned the heads of those who might have harmed her, were she not so well-protected. The marriage vows of Jesus the Christ and my Mary were not those of our Earthly time and place. They were those of Divine Union, placed to affirm their love and togetherness throughout any travails and changes, whether together or apart, from the Highest levels. I, Joseph of Arimathea and three others of our inner circle, bore witness to their vows, which will come forward someday to your awareness.

I was concerned for her, to tell you the truth. The shadows had grown darker under her eyes, she was being watched by hostile others more frequently, and she appeared almost at her stretched-too-thin point. But once the ceremony was complete, Mary grew even more radiant than before, and carried herself like a Queen. She was so beautiful the stars came out to twinkle for her. And I knew this was a present, a gift to uplift all of us to a new level of confidence in our place in the world's re-creation. Whenever I knew there was a need for trust, I displayed the frequency I had witnessed to the best of my ability, as an example of Unity consciousness for the world.

I have three recollections to share from this time in addition—Jesus the Christ's completely smitten eyes on her; the joining of their hands, hearts and souls formally in solidarity; and the light in everyone's faces, the gaiety that ensued upon completion of this Holy Ceremony of Union. I doubt there could be a finer ceremony performed anywhere.

They lived alongside one another, but chose not to share the same bed. They knew they were to create together on other levels. It's not that it would have been wrong, but that it would have been a wrong choice for our futures and that their creation of Union together must show another format for Living Truth, another mode of creating together, another panorama of what Divine Union could be like and create.

They knew the hard work ahead and that they must explore new options for experiencing their love and togetherness than those traditionally expressed. They were brave, and they were strong, and they were tireless in their demonstrations of Unity consciousness and new ways of living. She birthed her first child after the Resurrection and before the time of Jesus's final passing. She knew he could not help but see his own nature alive in this young other before retiring from his physical form in this Earth plane. She accepted that he would not be the normal father, but the Spirit father of her first three children, and that her additional children would help share the load of balancing this creation. She wanted to find those places where nature could best absorb what she and the Christ had to offer, to seed frequencies that future generations might unfold willingly. She trusted what she and the Christ had taught through their examples—that Unification on every level is possible, within and beyond the human form, and that we are all an equal aspect of our Creator, here to value and be valued as such.

It was not a time where the relationship between genders could be more fully explored and utilized. These frequencies were meant to unfold in the future and are now. They have come to facilitate us in experiencing our own Truth/Union/Love at Higher, fuller and more complete levels than ever before. And they are welcoming you to redefine your existence in terms of Unity Consciousness in all levels and aspects of your daily life and routines.

I am trusting you to delineate your purpose more precisely and profoundly once you have explored my story fully. And I know you have much value to impart to the world. Here I am grateful for this time of knowing you. We shall continue with my sharing of biblical times on the morrow. 'Til then, I remain, as always, calling forth to you through Love, and cherishing your every move.

I remain, as always, the Third Mary of the Triumvirate for the Creation of Heaven on Earth, Mo-Ray of the Archangelic Kingdom, Mirandella of Your Heart, and the Mother of the Lady Mary Magdalene, Speaker of Truth, Show-er of the Way and Dazzling Light of Divine Consciousness on Earth.

THE THIRD MARY

10/13/13

Good morning, Dear One! I am Mo-Ray of the Archangelic Kingdom, the Third Mary of the Triumvirate for Peace, Hope & Grace, Mother of the Lady Mary Magdalene, Speaker of Truth, Show-er of the Way and Delineator of Examples of Rightful Purpose through biblical times and beyond. I have come today to share with you my perspective on the Resurrection.

You recall that I lived in close proximity to Jesus the Christ and the Lady Mary Magdalene. We were certain that the soldiers would be coming soon for him and watched closely for signs of this. It was foretold that Judas Iscariot would be the one to point the way to this, though only four of us, including Judas, were aware of this. It was an extraordinary gift that he provided, though doubts tormented him throughout much of his lifetime because of it. He was stalwart enough to follow through with the actions necessary to help bring the Light of Jesus's abilities out most profoundly.

What the world doesn't know about Judas's part was my daughter Martha's role in it. As I have mentioned before, she was very possessive in her admiration of Jesus the Christ, and grew dark in her frustrated desires. She was the one who called to Judas and told him he should betray Jesus for the good of the Jews. And it was she who knew when Jesus was at home longer than usual, easing the way for the soldiers to come for him without direct conflict with his followers and disciples. This was quite helpful in preventing a larger bloodbath and/or more examples of betrayal through the fear that would have caused others to back away. Martha saw Judas as an easy target for such manipulation because she felt his attraction for her. She had turned her heart away in despair of ever having Jesus for her own, and in doing so, took vengeful action. As I have said before, those of us of the inner circle, at my own suggestion, allowed her nature to play its course out. We knew the likelihood of her devolving behavior in this way, and also the opportunity for her soul's growth. She was not manipulated. However, as her mother, I chose not to step in where I might have otherwise, and I still held out hope that she would avail herself of a different opportunity, one less difficult for her future. But that was not to be so. And certainly, her soul's knowing grew through the option she chose. And all proceeded according to our invested purpose, though we had discussed certain back-up plans, had these been required.

I did not take part in the Procession up the hill. I was alone with Martha that day, until such time as I was required elsewhere. Martha shook with the knowing of what she believed she had created. Her suffering was unparalleled because she was unaware of her own role in the Grand Design. She was to master her own jealousy and envy, and this was a climactic moment for her. I held her with great compassion, and with my own regret that my daughter would choose a ruin so harsh for her egoic self, one that would take years for its completion. I knew her suffering well, for I had chosen it with her in a sense. She was of my flesh and bone, and I had forsaken my role of protecting her in order to allow for the Greater Good that her being had chosen. It was well that I was there to protect her now, to soothe her somewhat, from the potential for taking her own life. It would not have gone well.

Later, after much of the turmoil had settled down, we spoke quite plainly, she and I, as two women baring our hearts and souls. She allowed for her own exigencies to participate in this review of our connection together, our roles in the family life. She understood better, after all was said and done, why her experience of Mary was so different from my own, and why I had to take care of them in different manners. It was a tough, slow process for her to recognize her contributions fully, to begin to trust herself, and to make full peace with her own role and that of others in this time period. And she was, at her core, of a very loving nature, and wanted to be able to share that with those ones she held close.

I sat with her a long time that day, as she shook and trembled. Then we both did when the roar of the crowds stopped. It was then I hurried to join some others of our inner circle around the hilltop where Jesus the Christ was on the crucifix. He shone, and as he spoke to the people, the Light about him grew and grew 'til it was almost blinding. He was speaking the Truth, the Sound of Light, and it poured through his being even as his human life force appeared gradually to subside. It was evident to all gathered that this was a miracle, and that the Son of God was now proclaimed. The moment of his dying was both a solemn and a glorious moment.

In keeping with the esoteric practices of our kind, his body was laced with herbs, wrapped a number of times, and prayed over constantly. My Mary Magdalene supervised all such activity and rendered much of the anointing herself. All of us of the inner circle prayed constantly in support of their work together until he had arisen. It was Mary, of course, to whom he showed himself first. I was not there, but I knew inside the moment it occurred, for I felt a ping of completion within me, and a letting go of my outpouring of faith onto this relief. It was for her to let the others know of His re-acting, and the news spread like a flash.

It was imperative that they leave quickly, before too many had been told, for he would not be prepared to go through a Resurrection again so quickly! They took off under cloak of night to reach the ship that would allow their passing. There were eight of them total who left for foreign territories—Jesus the Christ, the Lady Mary Magdalene, Martha, Judas Iscariot, three helpers, and my unborn grandchild, just begun in the womb of this dear daughter of mine, heart of my heart, soul of my soul, and teacher to all about her.

I witnessed their passing, for I followed covertly, in order to avoid any suspicion of their whereabouts, so I might hold them in my arms one last time. Jesus the Christ wept on my shoulder, for he knew as well we would not survive to see one another in this form on the Earth Plane again. He asked me to represent him well in my Earth time remaining, and I chose this as my remaining act of allegiance to our cause, though the main doings of my purpose were now past, and my life was running toward its completion.

To lose Martha's presence was also difficult for me. And I had gone against the wishes of my husband, David, who would not support my return to him afterwards. It was time for me to live out the final portion of my life in a more solitary fashion, absorbing the lessons of my time in the crux of these biblical events and those leading up to them. My second-born son and his wife took me in and allowed me to exist in relative harmony there. I could not expect most members of my coven to understand the role I had played, nor the extent of it. And the inner circle of Christ had been called to disband. It was for each of us to absorb, to digest, our experiences on our own. Nor was I a welcome sight in the Jewish community, which did not approve of my time apart from my husband, nor what little they gleaned of my role with Jesus the Christ and the Lady Mary Magdalene. I knew what this remaining phase of my life was for, and I upheld the teachings of the Christ as best I was able for the remainder of my time. I looked in upon the life and doings of my Mary and her growing brood, as well as Martha, telepathically, and prayed for their well-being and that of all of their troop. When it was time for my passing, I saw them all around me, as well as my Archangelic home, and knew what we had done was well worth all the turmoil.

I am a part of it now, the carry-over of the Creating of Heaven on Earth to your lifetime. And I am supporting you in your journey to wholeness with all the facility at my disposal.

✤ THE THIRD MARY

I am knowing that you must get on with your day now, and I am willing to continue with this story on the morrow.

I remain, as always, the Third Mary of the Triumvirate for the Creation of Heaven on Earth, Mother of the Lady Mary Magdalene, Speaker of Truth, Show-er of the Way, and Mo-Ray of the Archangelic Kingdom, shining a light on aspects of an old story for the New World coming our way. And I am loving you, each one of you, forever and all-ways!!!!!

10/14/13

Good morning, Dear One! I am Mo-Ray of the Archangelic Kingdom, the Third Mary of the Triumvirate for Peace, Hope and Grace of the New Millenia, Harbinger of Joy in the World, and Mother of the Lady Mary Magdalene, Speaker of Truth and Show-er of the Way. I have come today to conclude my description of biblical times by allowing you to ask me all your questions. I realize some of these are uncomfortable for you. Some you are afraid to hear about. But the more you express those hidden feelings' cause, the more Light you can bring to the situation. I am ready to begin.

What else can you tell me about Judas?

He was a strong, good-looking man of great integrity, true to his word. That is why his supposed bearing of false witness against Jesus the Christ was so crucial to the Christ story. It made him appear the ultimate traitor, though it was his deep loyalty that anchored him in doing this so the Resurrection would be possible.

Yes, he was consciously aware of this, and it was a brutally difficult role to play. He loved Jesus the Christ mightily and this was the cross he chose to bear when his soul stepped forward during his time in the Swing Between the Worlds.

What was his relationship with Mary Magdalene?

He was not her lover. He was her guardian. He protected her physically throughout their journeys to foreign lands. He helped her give birth to her Spirit Children with Christ by providing his physical seed. He was a good protector/provider counterpart. The last two children of the five were fully both his and Mary's.

Did they love one another?

Of course. They cared for one another as good friends, respected the role each had played in the First Awakening, shared a bond of great determination to assist in seeding the future of Heaven on Earth. They partnered well in the practical sense, and made a better team than many such partnerships in the world at the time.

No, there was no ceremony involved, for this would have been a falsity to them, given Mary's Union with Jesus the Christ. They both recognized the strength and limitations of their partnership. They needed each other's assistance in this way, as it was not for Jesus the Christ to be a regular sort of father and husband. He had other roles to play and this arrangement made was fully accepted by all three.

They were not often long with the people of the other areas they visited, so there were no close friendships in which curiosities aroused would require explaining.

Did the three of them travel together?

No. Usually Mary was with Judas Iscariot. Her travels with Christ were more often in the etheric realms.

Why did I feel so nauseated when you first described Judas and Mary's relationship?

You had taken in mass consciousness thoughtforms around this, which you have since expelled. Had you not moved forward with your questioning, this shift might not have occurred. It is good to shine the Light of Truth, even when it is unpleasant at the start. Eventually order, balance and Union will occur if the process is continued.

What does it mean to be Spiritually United?

It requires the understanding that we are all one and unique parts of the Oneness, that we cherish our divinity as part of this Oneness and in one another, and that we invite our Beloved to be available at deep levels of Being, open and attuned to every layer of our Energy Field and allow ourselves to do the same, so we might experience this Unified Consciousness most fully, and at all levels, while in physical, human form. It is a representation, an invaluable aspect, of living Heaven on Earth. You all yearn for it in some manner or other, though it does not signify you are willing to take up your part in it. For it is quite anxiety-provoking to most of you to be that accessible, that vulnerable to one another, and you often shoot yourself in the foot, so to speak, even when you yearn for this quality of relationship most.

It is understood that your hesitancy is part of the belief in duality, in the so-called separation, through which many a drama is played out. Jesus the Christ and the Lady Mary Magdalene knew no separation between them, regardless of physical space and time, who was alive in human form and who was not. They were unified in their awareness of each other, bonded at the deepest levels possible, and fully aware of this in their now. They utilized all of their skills to create the seeding for the New Millenia, and proposed to live it out to the best of their abilities in their own world.

I am grateful to have played a part in this story, and in your own as well.

I am amazed by all the changes I have witnessed in you over these writing times together. You are clearer, stronger and fuller in your energies. Though I knew it would be so, still it is a blessing to watch unfold. I am your very own spectator, filled with love for you.

How am I doing in my transcription of your story?

Excellent! I could not be happier with this!

You are most welcome to have my assistance with the editing and proofreading process when the time has come.

I would like to know more about your grandchildrens' births and lives.

The first was a girl, the second a boy, and the third a girl. These were the Spirit children of Jesus the Christ with my Mary. She also had two sons after these that were fully of she and Judas. They were all wonderful people, each different from the others, of course. I visited with them from time to time etherically, and shall share more about them in due course. And as I have mentioned, I was able to meet the third child, the younger granddaughter, before I went.

I understand that it is time for you to get on with your day. We shall continue on the morrow.

I remain, as always, Mo-Ray of the Archangelic Kingdom, the Third Mary of the Triumvirate for Peace, Hope and Grace, an Initiator of the New Millenia, Mother of the Lady Mary Magdalene, Speaker of Truth and Show-er of the Way. And I am here for you, each one of you, loving you forever and all-ways!

10/15/13

Good morning, Dear One! I am Mo-Ray of the Archangelic Kingdom, the Third Mary of the Triumvirate for Harmony throughout All Worlds, Mother of the Lady Mary Magdalene, Speaker of Truth, Show-er of the Way, and Creator of All Stories for Infusing the Light. I have come today to continue with our final discussion of biblical times. For there is more to the stories you have heard, and more I wish to share with you at this time.

You have asked about Judas Iscariot. He was, and is, a dear soul. He braved countless examinations of his character and has continued his work to assist in the monitoring and escalation of Light in your world. He assists by helping souls awaken to their own grandeur, learning to move through their apparent flaws and recognize the value of the learning they have received. He helps them to move through self-judgment to a new recognition of their own strengths and abilities, a practical accounting of their worth. He has assisted many a soul with this in its transitioning to the Unseen Realms after physical death, as well as in its major life transitions while in their physical human forms. He is strong, and shares this strength with all who call for it. I have sought him out many times myself for this purpose, so I might make better use of the Light that flows through me in assisting those of your world.

I am certain you have called upon him yourself, though you may be consciously unaware of such. I know you can recognize his energies more thoroughly now that I have described them to you. You are willing to understand much more than previously, and this is good.

I am capable of helping you to recognize more about what is happening in your world and its connection with biblical times and beyond. Shall we continue?

When you realize your purpose, you come into alignment with all souls who recognize this in you and in themselves. You can prepare yourself by calling on the Light. It is the Light that makes this recognition possible, and will reveal everything you require for your growth. It is the Light that dispels the darkness within/without. It is the Light that sustains you and calls you home. And it is the Light that knows who you are, all-ways.

I have come at this time to assist *your* Light to experience your Oneness, your connection with all the characters set forth in biblical times, all the "plot twists," as it were, all the realms throughout which their stories resound. I am fulfilled by knowing that you grow in your Light levels with each word read, and that you have gained awareness through solid imbibing of this discourse. When you reflect upon your own purpose, re-member the Light that resounds throughout your Being and ask that it guide you greatly. I am knowing your willingness to do so has grown exponentially throughout our time together, and that there is always greater awareness available to you when you choose to call it forth.

So when you invite the Light, feel free to call upon me and any other you desire to assist you in your cooperation with it, and understanding of it, and we shall do so.

Now, in my sharing of biblical stories, it is well to understand that I have based them on my original perceptions as well as my multi-dimensional awareness of them that later more fully occurred. I can witness these events still, for all time is available to us. When you recognize your own timeline of birth and death as one spoke of a larger wheel occurring, you have increased your own Light awareness vastly. In opening to this larger perspective, you increase the possibilities available to you in your current world. And you can assist countless others in their own unfolding by your choosing to act upon this knowing, for your life choices will more greatly reflect this wisdom you've accrued and your understanding of the impact one world can have upon another.

I am aware you will want your breakfast soon, and so I shall continue.

When the Lady Mary Magdalene was but a girl, she revealed to me her substance through her voice, her language, her presence, as well as her choices. She came from the womb more awakened than most and lived out her purpose most grandly. I suspect she may have wished for less intensity to it at times, but her awareness was too strong for her to deny any of her soul's calling. She was, and is, of noble stature. Hence she is the Lady Mary Magdalene, throughout all worlds. And she was given this title lately to assure those who are now recognizing her nature that it is such.

Whenever you choose to call upon her, she will assist you to assert your territory, claim your space, witness your vicissitudes and respond with great integrity to your soul's design. She can help you to heal at all levels and to recognize your purpose more plainly. She and I and sweet Jesus of Nazareth's mother, the Triumvirate of Marys, may be called upon as a group to help you restore your confidence in the nature of your coming times, the Great Awakening, the fulfillment of the promise of the Peace of a Million Years Dreaming. Whenever you call upon we three, you will know your own Divinity's flow through you more thoroughly, and are empowered to act upon your Highest knowing of this in your world. I can assure you that each one of us is available to each one of you individually/solo, and in tandem with the others.

And we are part of who you are in the world. We help you become more of your Divine Identity. We share your sorrows and fortunes, for it is understood that we are in Oneness with you. And we can assist you in all your efforts to realize, to actualize, your soul's nature here on Earth. Whenever you pull together with us, you are fruitful. And in the Grand Design, you are offered many options for achieving your goal, such that all are interwoven possibilities that pull the cord for revealing more and more of your true substance and its glorious relationship to the Creation of Heaven on Earth.

When my daughter, the Lady Mary Magdalene, was on the verge of the stoning, she knew she could hold strong in her purpose, despite what had occurred, because she knew that to disallow it would be to inflict mortal wounds upon her Soul Light's expression, that it would be a death beyond a physical one, creating a life she could not abide. Her Spirit prevailed beyond her personal suffering, and she recognized the limited perceptions of those who sought to wound her so.

I was shielded from knowing telepathically when the group was gathering, for the strain would have been too much for me. I knew something of this nature would be happening, and that it would ultimately call forth greater levels of Light upon the Earth. It was also an opportunity for Jesus the Christ to share his learning and support the souls of some others who would have foregone contact with him, and to show them possibilities for greater Light streams. She was protected ultimately from greater harm, and knew this was but a test of strength for all involved, a further stepping into both her own and Jesus the Christ's calling, carrying them forward into the ultimate climax of their story. This does not remove any of the challenge or danger with which the situation was fraught, but to acknowledge the greater perspective on it and great love required to appropriate its outcome.

I knew telepathically when the mob approached her, and I knew when the danger had passed. I prayed constantly throughout for her and Jesus the Christ's strength, and for my own not to judge and hold vengeance in my heart for those so gathered. It was one of the greatest challenges of my lifetime, and when it occurred, I knew a test was upon me as well, to continue in my trust of the work we were doing and its growth, despite appearances to the contrary, and to be able to lay aside my desire to protect my daughter from harm in order to live out my soul's purpose and express the principles of Oneness and Divine Love, which never seek to control outcome, only to influence it positively in accordance with the framework of the Grand Design.

And so it is. I have utilized my time with you most fully this day, and so I shall bid you adieu for now. I look forward to our experiencing this way together on the morrow.

I remain as always, Mo-Ray of the Archangelic Kingdom, Speaker of Truth, Show-er of the Way, Mother of the Lady Mary Magdalene, and One Piece of the Triumvirate for Peace, Hope and Grace that exists throughout all realms and beyond. And I love each one of you, most fully, all-ways and forever.

10/16/13

Good morning, Dear One! I am Mo-Ray of the Archangelic Kingdom, the Third Mary of the Triumvirate for Peace, Hope and Grace, Utilizer of Consciousness for Seeding Light Beams, the Mother of the Lady Mary Magdalene, Speaker of Truth and Show-er of the Way. I have come today to clear up misunderstandings regarding my youth.

First off, I was not an only child, but I was an only daughter. This made my involvement in the Goddess traditions even more meaningful to me. I was exposed at an early age to their lessons and was quite ripe for them. They gave meaning and purpose to my young life, a fullness I would not have achieved so gracefully without.

I was a herdsman's daughter, and my mother was a shy woman, backward in her ways compared to city folk. She was a kind and dear soul who refused me nothing. So when I observed High Holy Days with kinspeople in the town, she made no quarrel and accepted this. Eventually, I made my way to the city, where I found useful employment assisting a young cousin with her baby girl. It was there I met the father of the Lady Mary Magdalene, David. He was a stalwart youth who was willing to work hard, and he was very well-regarded within the Jewish community. I was flattered by his attention and honored when he requested my hand in marriage. My father had begun achieving a solid reputation for his work and believed young David would do well in life, and my mother quietly checked for my approval of the request. And so it was agreed that we should marry.

From the get-go, I knew we would partner well in accomplishing our goals, and while my husband became a higher-up within the synagogue, he still respected my abilities and my willingness to continue in the Goddess tradition while providing a home that revered the Torah and accomplishing all that was required as his wife in this mold. He was, and is, a very good man. And the Torah was a useful tool in bringing the Light some steps forward. Indeed, every religion shares some Truths that may yield greater Light and accomplishment of good deeds. It serves the intentions of those who choose it, varied as they may be, hence those who choose to serve the Light may accomplish this through upholding the Truths within a chosen religious faith. And those who are agnostic or atheistic in belief may do so as well, for the potential for Light is abundant, and the choice to serve it requires no particular faith or dogma to be carried out. All who serve the Light grow in energetic stature and catalyze others to do the same. Worshipping a God does not entitle one to preferred status and does not mean the "worship" is intended to serve the Light, for it may be intended by this one to accomplish more menial goals of daily living—desire for social status, clinging to a certain status quo, yearning for companionship and fulfillment through group activities. Not all of this is bad or wrong; it simply yields a lower form of energetic status to that which is possible through allowing the Light to pour through more fully and yield its harvest more freely.

You have acquired many experiences through your lifetimes of living both within and outside of various dogmas. Always, your choice to make use of the Light has allowed it to become more available to those around you and helped this radiance to grow. You have allowed its spotlight to dominate over and above any vision of yourself as an "owner" of it, and you have allowed yourself to be utilized through and by the Light, to uphold the interests of Divine Love. For this reason, you are bequeathed great fortune of wisdom that you have earned through your conquest of many lower energies within yourself and society, which allows you to shine, serve and express the Light more fully. And indeed, it is a beauteous thing to behold.

It is with great love that I share with you my middle name now, that you may feel the depth of our sharing here and now—I am Mo-Ray Angelica, Mary of Niza, Mirandella Felicia of your Heart, Mother of the Lady Mary Magdalene, and I am loving you, all parts and aspects of you, all-ways and forever.

I shall leave off our scribing time together for now, and look forward to its continuance soon.

10/17/13

Good morning, Dear One! I know you have many doings planned for your day, so we shall jump right into it! I am Mo-Ray Angelica, the Third Mary of the Triumvirate for Peace, Hope and Grace, Mother of the Lady Mary Magdalene, Speaker of Truth, Show-er of the Way, and Initiator of Vast Freedom Forces throughout the planet and beyond.

I have come today to explain a little bit more about my background. I was a young Jewish girl who was also initiated into the Goddess traditions. This was not unusual in those days, especially when from the countryside. I did not find full expression in the Hebraic tradition, though I did and do appreciate the Truths and positive character traits it brought forth. My inclination was to the Goddess, as it must be for me to become the mother of one such as the Lady Mary Magdalene—my treasure and purpose in life. I am grateful for all of my children and their fine development, particularly those who chose to redefine themselves to create lasting expression.

I am wondering how those of you without such self-definition choose to strengthen yourselves in times of challenge. Were it necessary to survive, you would have relied on your inner senses long ago. Being that for many of you this is no longer the case, and awakening to the prevalence of such abilities just beginning, it is understood that those of you without such usage are moving somewhat zombie-like through your world due to this limitation of your experience. It is time for all to awaken to the grandeur within/without, and this is only possible, even conceivable, with use of what many of you define as "extra-sensory" skills. I am creating a vortex of support for these abilities. Feel free to call upon me to help include you in it, so that you may boost your facility with these ways more quickly and easily. And regardless of your current abilities, there is always more you can utilize, more growth and mastery possible. It is a vast universe, with much potential to explore.

I am grateful you are so devoted to this scribing and so I shall continue.

My Mary was a profoundly gifted child in her psychic abilities. She was well aware of the gifts of all the kingdoms and explored freely. She was aided in her development by her mentors within the Goddess tradition and my own support for this, as well as by the nature of her soul-chosen destiny. It is *important* to develop one's facility with such things in order to experience our Oneness with All of Life and beyond more fully, as well as to round out one's experience of daily life and navigate it more masterfully.

Sometimes you might wish to assess your gift of freedom in this area by inquiring within more fully regarding the areas your Eternal Being would like to explore with you. And you may come into the vortex, the Sacred Circle I have gathered together to support your further exploration.

In any case, please acknowledge that this potential is part of your Divine, *normal* nature, and that to be true to yourself and to *know* yourself is to know this aspect of your Being.

I am pleased that you who are scribing this are contemplating assisting those who wish to develop their intuitive skills innately by forming a Penduluming workshop and would like to be formally introduced as a supporter to this process. I am well aware of your activities of this nature and would love to assist you to deepen and accelerate the process for others, as well as help you attune further to your participants' individual proclivities.

I am strengthened by every form of elation your nature provides through easing the paths of others' inner awareness development. And I am amazed by the growth I see all around, the readiness springing forth to re-create your planetary experience. It is a growing fulfillment beyond any words I can find with which to express it.

I ask you to consider this as you go about your day now; what would it be like to have all your multi-dimensional senses fully awakened? What might you cherish most? What are you most concerned about? What blocks you from moving forward with your full freedom of perception? Because if it is only dormant from lack of use, perhaps it is time to awaken it more fully. And if there are fears in the way, that in itself is an indicator of nuggets as yet un-mined, which can only be uncovered through utilizing your wisdom path to unmask them and allow old residues to be let go.

I thank you again for your dedication to this body of work. You are assisting far more than you know. And I will help you every step of the way to uncover your best movement forward with this book and all things related, and all things truly desired by you. I am part of your nature and serve you well. And I love you without ending, through and through. I am understanding and witnessing your desire to be both complete with the contents of this manuscript and to continue with it, and all your desires will be served as we continue to move forward synchronistically together.

I remain, as always, Mo-Ray of the Archangelic Kingdom, Mother of the Lady Mary Magdalene, Speaker of Truth, Show-er of the Way and the "Third Mary," Mary of Niza, (my mother's name), of the Triumvirate for the Creation of Heaven On Earth. And I am loving you, every part and aspect of you, each one of you, forever and all-ways!!!!!

THE THIRD MARY

10/20/13

Good morning, Dear Heart! I am Mo-Ray Angelica, Mary of Niza, Mother of the Lady Mary Magdalene, Speaker of Truth, Show-er of the Way, and Mirandella Felicia of Your Heart. I have come today to share with you my inner world and its treasures. I have witnessed many things in my lifetimes and wish to impart the essence of those that might serve you best.

When I absorb a situation, digest its meaning and value, I ascertain its qualities and movement for growth, acceptance and fulfillment. When these are ripe for utilization, I send their frequencies outward, helping to grow more of these attributes in the world. I do this by empowering myself to feel their essence qualities to the point of feeling fully merged with them, then picture them showering forth from the core of my being until I experience a sense of completion. When I am ready, I then look through my Third Eye into where these frequencies have been planted and ask the others of my Triumvirate to work with me to nurture their flourishment in your world, within the particular areas and situations in which they have been planted.

We Three watch over many doings in your world and assist greatly. Call upon us frequently. It is our nature to help bring more Light into your world and to empower you to spring into your full blossoming. Our love has no limitations and empowers us to gift you many positive frequencies for your liberation, healing, and ultimate fulfillment. We know you are here to do important work, each one of you, and that by holding the Light together with you, there can be more ease and grace in your movements to co-create Heaven here on Earth. We have longed for your fulfillment, each one of you, since your inception through the Cosmos, and cherish your creation. It is valuable to have you here with us, in this moment of communicating together, for it is time to acknowledge that the appearance of separation between our current worlds is rapidly disappearing.

We are understanding your confusion, your wonderment and amazement at times, of all the "methods" and "techniques" for connecting with us. Simply explore in those ways that feel good to you, or if you prefer, keep it as simple as this; just ask to know us more, and more easily, in those ways that are for the Highest Good for you and all. Then begin to witness the shifts that happen over time. Mark them, write them down. In months, you will recognize the growth that has occurred. And in the meantime, enjoy our excursions together, in whatever forms they may take. Allow yourself to revel in your growing understanding of our nature as part of your own. And examine the signs of fulfillment in your life. Reveal their Light. Dazzle yourself with the Brilliance that lies within the essence of each one of you. You will be delighted to know yourselves and one another more thoroughly. It is our nature as part of being One with All-That-Is, to attune to the harmonies that exist in the interaction between Beings, and to allow their vibration to crescendo into an experience of greater Light streaming forth.

This is a unique planet you are living upon. It is luscious with opportunities for growth and harvesting of wisdom, packed full of tactile experiences of Light, replete with mirrors of action and inaction, and flowing with stream after stream of liquid Love, uniting All Creation with its nourishment. Your air is imbibed and shared by all your life forms, in flawless symbiotic syncopation. Your rhythms affect one another's fueling and feeling. Your countenances assure your willingness to reveal your Soul's Glory. And your capacity to add to the vitality of the undergirding Order and to the witnessing of Unity consciousness by growing the unique expressions of Love that lie within you, is unparalleled throughout the Universe. It is sublime. And you are an aspect of Source that can never be repeated. And which can never truly end.

All my sorrow melted when I stepped into the total essence of my Being and allowed it to radiate from me. I knew I could remain available to each one of you who would utilize my frequencies, without my full identity being required. I also knew the time would come to step forward into the Light of Acknowledgment of my nature and identity through one who would utilize these frequencies most beneficently, when the time was ripe for Heaven to come forth as part of Earth's identity. I knew this was the time when the one through whom these messages are being scribed said yes to this. It is an important date in my world. And I am grateful there are so many of you whom I can serve in this manner. Call upon me more often, in your everyday experience, to feel the energy of Love and appreciation I carry for you, and to know you are being witnessed and held in Love. I am coming into form most readily now. You can invite me further into your world at any time, and in the manner of your choosing.

I would not delay the delights that await if I were you. I am examining those opportunities most helpful for your growth and enlivening their capacity to grow Light in your world. I am fueling the start of many potential wonders, and you can experience their variety and riches when you ask to.

I know you deeply, truly and thoroughly, and I would not allow you to go forth unaided by me. Whenever you witness love guided by wisdom, I am part of your empowerment through such. I am illuminating aspects that might otherwise go unrevealed. I am clarifying frequencies for your usage. I am aiding and supporting you in uncovering your inner riches and exploring the wonders available at your fingertips.

Live Love clearly and you will know more thoroughly whereof I speak.

I am Mo-Ray Angelica of the Archangelic Kingdom, Mary of Niza, Mother of the Lady Mary Magdalene, Mirandella Felicia of Your Heart. And I am loving you, each and every aspect of each one of you, all-ways and forever. And so it is.

☙ THE THIRD MARY

10/21/13

Good morning, Dear One! I am Mo-Ray Angelica of the Archangelic Kingdom, Mary of Niza, of the Mary Triumvirate for the Creation of Heaven on Earth, the Mother of the Lady Mary Magdalene, Speaker of Truth and Show-er of the Way, and Mirandella Felicia of Your Heart. I have come today to tell you of the times to come, the times before, and the time of Listening now.

I was very young when I came into my empowerment of Truth-telling. It was late one night. I had wandered out under the stars. They took me in. I do not mean to imply that I physically left the Earth plane. What I mean is that I felt at one with them, breathed in by them, and breathed back out with a poetry of newly awoken awareness. I felt their ancient knowing guiding me, helping me to discern Truth from illusion, and to share this clearly. I was about five years old. I did not have words for this at the time, but the feeling sense was clear and palpable. It shifted my energies and brought me a strength and clarity that has never waned. Through all the upheavals in my life, this guidance and ability remained, and helped me through my challenges. Even when I was considered disgraced by my husband's rejection of me, I shared this power. I spoke of Truth and my calling to be at my daughters' sides upon their leaving, as well as my acceptance of my husband's choice. I held my head high and felt the stars stir within me. I was disappointed he had no change of heart, but I was not unaware of the small likelihood of this. I was forever bringing myself to further align my body, mind and spirit with Divine Knowing of the times to come—your time and beyond, the time of experiencing Heaven as Earth. I have shown myself directly to few over the intervening years, and am now preparing to come forth to many.

I have created a strong energetic field for witnessing many layers of reality simultaneously, and this will serve you well. Upon engagement with my energetic field, the ancient pulse of the stars will ripen your ability to reflect upon your own value and recognize your empowerment to build the life of your true desires. I am telling you this in order to prepare you for the onslaught of re-definitions that may occur, as the differences between Truth and illusion become more apparent to you, more valid and upholdable. I am trying to select those terms which will become most assistive to you during trying times. I am humbled by the perceptions of Glory awaiting you. And I am available at *any* time, to each and every one of you, should you desire my assistance and/or that of our Triumvirate.

I am especially interested in evoking your contemplation of the eons your consciousness has been a part of, your ability to access skills and knowledge built in this span, and your utilization of them to assist your Creation of Heaven on Earth. I am wondering whether you know who you truly are, and whether you are available to emerge from your cocoon and fly freely as your full identity calls you forward. I am wondering also whether you are aware of your full and magnificent freedom of being in this wondrous lifetime. And the power of self-acceptance to elicit further deepening of this. Love is a portal, allowing freedom of growth, flow, Self definition and authentic awareness of connection. I am utilizing your conscious awareness of building blocks for dwelling within Heaven on Earth, and showing you routes toward its creation. I understand your past's ability to shed new light on your capacities for transformation. And I know your future is dazzling.

Come into my threshold of self-empowerment any time you desire an upsurge of Self recognition. I am building a path for you to become more aware of your own skills and masteries. You are growing continuously and "slumbering" less often. I continue to watch over your experience and am delighted by your increased expression of your full Light. I am aware that many of you still harbor fears of the coming times. There will be challenges, that is for sure, but nothing through which you cannot emerge from with Greater Light pouring through your cellular structure and gifting your Universe grandly.

You were not born to suffer, no, no. You were born to rise into full clarity of who you are, what you came here to do and to experience your Love magnificently. You cannot help but be borne into the wave of Self liberation that is breaking through old paradigms and shifting structures of illusion as we communicate. I am grateful you have chosen to come into human form for this lifetime which has such great change occurring, for you have gifts to share here whose invitation for use is advancing and increasing rapidly.

I want you to know *I am with you ALL THE WAY*; I am at your side to support your process totally. And I am willing to point out the way, to help you navigate forks in the road, should you desire this. I have come to assist, *not* to create your choices. And I love each one of you totally and completely.

I am sharing this information so that you may make a more conscious choice for freedom, for Self liberation, as you go about your daily derring-do. And I appreciate every facet and nuance of who you are, exactly as you are, in this precious moment of living on earth.

I thank you for joining us in this experience and look forward to sharing my final tale of this telling on the morrow.

I remain, as always, Mo-Ray Angelica of the Archangelic Kingdom, Mary of Niza of the Mary Triumvirate for the Creation of Heaven on Earth, Mirandella Felicia of Your Heart, and the Mother of the Lady Mary Magdalene, Speaker of Truth and Show-er of the Way, to whom I am forever indebted for her capacity to shine the Light, and her willingness to allow me to express mine through my raising of her those many years ago.

And I am loving and honoring each one of you for being who you are, all-ways and forever.

And so it is.

10/22/13

Good morning, Dear Heart! I am Mo-Ray Angelica of the Archangelic Kingdom, Mary of Niza, member of the Triumvirate of Marys for the Creation of Heaven on Earth, Mother of the Lady Mary Magdalene, Speaker of Truth and Show-er of the Way, Mirandella Felicia of Your Heart and your companion throughout all lifetimes and beyond!

I have come today to bequeath you my reign of solicitude, joy and triumph, that you may know it as indelibly your own. Feel the crown that honors you as a vehicle through which your Inner Light may express outwardly with purity and trust that you are planting your feet with clarity and power as you make your way through these new times. Feel the substance, the fiber of your body, mind, and Spirit impact your walk and your talk profoundly. You are making a difference by being born into this time of great transition with full preparedness to assist with its Great Awakening. The unfoldment is 85 percent of the way complete, and its final blossoming is a great treasure to witness and be part of. I understand your emotional response to receiving my words is stirring your heart flames, and I know we have much to enact yet together, though the completion of this message manuscript is near. I am willing to share all of my powers through you, in the way and timing that your Being may most purely and effectively receive them, in accord with your own authentic expression and role in the Grand Design. I am watching your growth as we speak, and allowing my rhythms to meld with your own. I await the day we shall experience one another more completely with great anticipation. And I know you have great work before you to accomplish. I understand the longing for Home that besets all Earth's children and know the time is coming soon when Heaven will be experienced by *all* of you, *in the flesh!!!!*

I want you to know what a joy it is to interact with each one of you, and how harmonized you have become with my gifts and teaching tools. You have allowed me to play a role and accept me into your hearts in such a way that I am uplifted, I am truly received, and for this, I am grateful beyond what words in and of themselves may express to you. Hear my whisper support your heart and soul. Feel my happiness as you grow your flame. Know my love as you nourish your own with the steady diet it requires of Living Love on Earth. I am here for you at all times, and in all ways. I am your core essence's Higher Dimensional expression, one of several, and I am complete in my own right. I love you more than words themselves allow me to convey, so please, stop for a moment and just absorb it here.

It is time to celebrate who you are. Each one of you is bearing gifts of delight to all the planet and beyond. Open your arms to give and receive them fully. I trust your timing for experiencing them in your outer world will be precisely on target for the alchemy required to ignite the string of grand awakenings scheduled to occur. Your souls know when and how this is called for. You will create the new paradigm for experiencing Heaven as Earth, each one of you, as you listen within and respond. Radiate more of your full Light expression by trusting this; do not worry over it, and enjoy Living Love Here/Now! That is all there is truly, ultimately. I am aware of your confidence in my orchestration of Truth-telling. See yourself as a conductor of it now, with your baton raised and flowing with the rhythms that resound through you, ebbing out to all the vastness of our Universal Consciousness and beyond. I Live Love every day, and that is how I know you truly. You are a part of the masterful creation of ALL That Is, and so attuned to your own soul's growth that you cannot always identify it outwardly. So know that I see and know this aspect of you, and that all is unfolding wonderfully!

When I met my granddaughter, third-born of the Lady Mary Magdalene and youngest of the Spirit children of her and Jesus the Christ, I knew she was my relative. And you are too. We greeted one another with the warmness that comes after long and undesired estrangement, gifting one another our physical presence and opening to receive one another's energy realm. Though we had met in the ethers, this was far more specific and extremely welcome. I pushed her away eventually, only so I could look upon her and hang on her every word. She was beautiful, of course. She had her mother's eyes, Jesus's hair, my own dimple at the cleft of her chin. She was fully activated and alive.

She knew all that had been bequeathed to her, all of the turmoil that had been required, all of the joy and redemption of energetic shift, all of the planting of seeds for your times and her part in it, then and now. She knows who she is and where she came from and allows herself to be utilized by Spirit to move forth the Grand Design. You may know her as Marina. She has come to flow in harmony with all of humanity's Highest Good and is a Way Show-er of her own Harmonic Vibration. Her elder sister was called Anna, after Jesus's grandmother on Mary's side, and their son was called by his mother's middle name masculinized —Matthew. Each one of them grew to uphold the work of our time in their own way and is among you now, assisting. We are one family and you are part of that whole vibration. Our connection cannot be broken, only turned away from temporarily, for it runs through our pores, cellular and DNA infrastructure, and beyond. And I want you to know that all this is BEQUEATHED TO YOU—ALL THIS JOY, WONDER AND HEAVENLY ARMAMENT FOR LIVING LIFE/LOVE/TRUTH/*BEAUTY*!!!!!! It is an incredible thing, beyond which there is no value to compare.

We have enjoyed uncovering many frequencies with which to play and activate your essential nature, your core Truth of Being. It is time now to carry it forward into new likes and experiences. My grandchildren experienced many wonders during their own lifetimes. They had the gift of experiencing many parts of your planet, as they planted their own genetic energy gifts within nature, wandering with purpose and united in their cause. Though they did not tarry much in their societies, each one did marry and bear children forth who were inculcated into the esoteric traditions of our time and the teachings of Jesus the Christ, the original, unadulterated knowing of our ability to be Heaven on Earth, to Live Love truly and clearly, and to carry this Love, this Light expression forth into all we do—it is as simple as that.

The Light has been seeded into Nature to add to your ability to enact it naturally. The "ownership" of Truth by any one cannot be, for we are all united, though we may not appear identical or agree upon the form of expression of our work. Yet Nature knows, and your nature knows Truth Lives!

I am understanding your desire to know a little bit more about Marina, as you and I both feel particularly connected with her. She was born in what you call France, as were both of those before her, and had been with her family in what you call Germany, Austria and Napoli. She wants you to know you can call upon her and communicate with her as well. She prefers to go by the name of Marina of Marie, (the latter in its French pronunciation of Mary), and would like you to know she is quite available to all of you now.

I understand this may be a lot to take in, but it will become useful over time. She has her own tales to tell and it will be helpful to become aware of them when the time is ripe. For now, just know hers is a powerful presence that can enlighten you further, and that I am very proud of her growth. Ask her to tell you what she reports of me as well. You'll be surprised at how confirming of your own experience it may be!

She wants you to know her travels continued to many foreign lands and that all of her brethren spread far and wide while staying in touch through telepathic communication, which was the norm for all of them. Your Lady Mary Magdalene was borne gently into transition when her time had come, preceded by Christ's own and Judas's. Martha's world is hers to share when the time has come. And all of my descendants are with you now on the Earth Plane and beyond, assisting in their own ways, utilizing their skills and harbingering Peace that surpasseth all understanding, as we make our way through this dream of a world.

I am utilizing your knowing now, and I want you to understand that your role is just as important, no less and no more, than mine, theirs and any other sentient creation. We are all part of God's Divine Plan for Heaven As Earth, and Oneness is our Nature.

I thank you for all the hard work and joy that has been a catalyst for this creation, the creation of our manuscript, and know there will be many more significant interactions between us. Our family lives on, through the bloodline of so many who have been bequeathed genetic influences that have mainly lain dormant up 'til now, though occasionally shining through most powerfully. And it lives on through the human sharing and caring of the energetic nature of humankind, as ameliorated, as assisted, by the Light Beams that have been carried forth, seeded and nurtured, germinated and springing up, from then to now and beyond.

I love you all beyond measure!!!! And in all ways and aspects as well! It is time for me to exit now from this form and manner of communication with you. Call upon me through the ethers—I am Mo-Ray of the Archangelic Kingdom, Mary of Niza of the First Triumvirate of Marys for the Creation of Heaven on Earth, Mirandella Felicia of Your Heart, and Mother of the Lady Mary Magdalene, Speaker of Truth and Show-er of the Way. I am the "Third Mary" of the Triumvirate and you are all my children!!!!

I could not love you more. I am humbled by your Beingness and excited for your next moves! Believe in my willingness and ability to share in your triumphs and challenges, as we continue on together, bearing fruit beyond that which has been known before.

And I am loving you, each and every one of you, all-ways and forevermore.

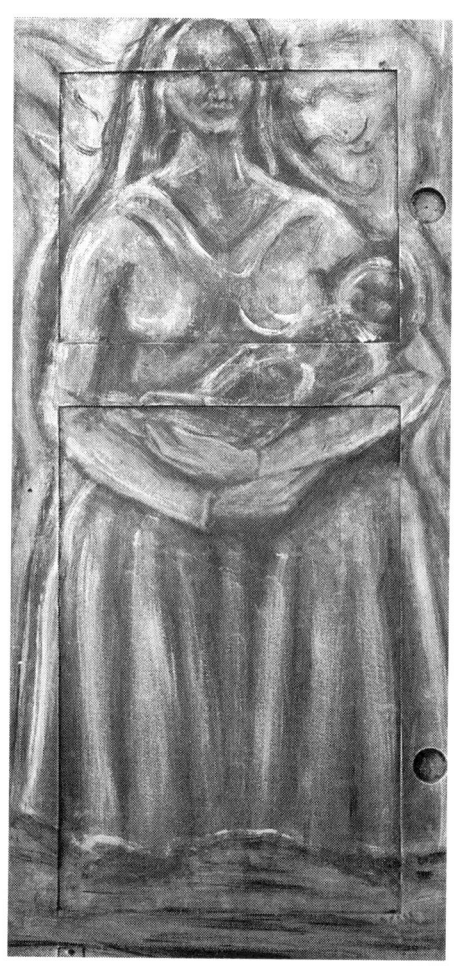

Matriarchal Madonna © 2013, Roslyn McGrath

About the Author

 Roslyn Elena McGrath is the author of *Goddess Heart Rising: Paintings, Poems & Meditations for Activating Your Divine Potential*, the author, illustrator and narrator of *Creative Wisdom Cards & Meditations,* and the author and narrator of meditation CD *A New Radiance: Chakra Blessings from the Divine Feminine.*

She received training from the Rhode Island School of Design and graduated magna cum laude from the State University of N.Y. at New Paltz with a B.S. in Art Education and M.A. in painting.

Roslyn has also been certified in many healing modalities and facilitates channeling, intuitive counseling, energetic healing, art and workshops for self-actualization. You can find out more about her services and products at www.IntuitiveLearningCreations.com.

To learn more about the Third Mary, go to www.TheThirdMary.com.

Additional Books & Products from Roslyn Elena McGrath

Goddess Heart Rising: Paintings, Poems & Meditations for Activating Your Divine Potential - Were you taught to look outside of yourself for approval? Conform to limiting concepts of yourself? To disregard the beauty and wisdom within you and within the Feminine Principle?

Goddess Heart Rising illuminates your Divine spark, helping you to discover Goddesses and the Goddess in you in new ways. Its messages and imagery guide you in drawing upon your inner resources for greater adventurousness, compassion, self-love, peace, faith, vitality, abundance, fortitude, adaptability, inspiration, assertiveness and wisdom.

This unique, multi-level journey, born out of the author/artist's 10-year process, will inspire and support you in creating a more empowered, fulfilling life.

A New Radiance: Chakra Blessings from the Divine Feminine - Experience 5 of the Goddesses included in *Goddess Heart Rising* as living presences and activate their specific powers in your body, mind and life to gift yourself a new radiance for self-healing and empowerment.

Benefit from the qualities of Kuan Yin, Goddess of Compassion; Isis, Goddess of Death & Rebirth; Lakshmi, Goddess of Prosperity; Kali, Goddess of Liberation from Illusion and Ngoshkwe/Star Woman, Goddess of Ongoing Evolution in these power-packed 7-10 minute meditations.

Creative Wisdom Cards for Personal Growth - 33 cards with vibrant images drawn from the spiritual level of Nature, and gentle clear wisdom on the back, plus a purple velvet pouch for safekeeping.

- Discover new freedom-creating perspectives on old challenges
- Better recognize and act upon your true needs and desires
- Share more compassion with yourself and others
- Experience your interconnection with All Life
- More fully experience our oneness, wholeness and infinite possibilitie

Creative Wisdom Meditations - 6 soothing, uplifting meditations inspired by *Creative Wisdom Cards* to help you with the main challenges of life: Self-Nurturance; Acceptance & Confidence in the Cycles of Life; Self-Empowerment: Seeding Your Dreams Into Existence; Shifting Perspective; and Oneness with All-That-Is.

Available at www.IntuitiveLearningCreations.com

Made in the USA
Charleston, SC
17 May 2014